The Management
of Ministry

The Management of Ministry

James D. Anderson

Ezra Earl Jones

1817

Published in San Francisco by

HARPER & ROW, PUBLISHERS

New York, Hagerstown, San Francisco, London

The Management of Ministry. Copyright © 1978 by
James D. Anderson and Ezra Earl Jones. All rights reserved.
Printed in the United States of America. No part of this
book may be used or reproduced in any manner whatso-
ever without written permission except in the case of brief
quotations embodied in critical articles and reviews. For
information address Harper & Row, Publishers, Inc., 10
East 53rd Street, New York, N.Y. 10022. Published simultaneously in Canada by Fitzhenry & Whiteside Limited,
Toronto.

Designed by Michael A. Rogondino

Library of Congress Cataloging in Publication Data

Anderson, James Desmond.
    THE MANAGEMENT OF MINISTRY.

    Bibliography: p. 199
    Includes index.
    1. Church management.   2. Clergy—Office.
3. Pastoral theology. I. Jones, Ezra Earl,
joint author. II. Title.
BV652.A67   1978   254   76–62942
ISBN 0–06–060235–X

78 79 80 81 82 10 9 8 7 6 5 4 3 2 1

254.8
An5

Baker & Taylor

Contents

Preface   vii

6. 27

18 Sept. 79

58742

Preface

The church carries out its ministry as it interprets and relates the Christian faith to the lives of individuals and groups, and to communities that encompass both. By assisting people in their role as worshippers to become more fully human, the church enables members of society to attain personal fulfillment and to respond to the real human needs of their communities.

In each generation and each place, the church seeks to redefine its reason for being, reexamine its fundamental task, understand the culture and concerns of its constituency, and work out methods for accomplishing its task. When it succeeds, people's lives and entire societies are enriched. When it fails, the church becomes weak and disintegrates, and society weakens with it.

Evaluated by statistical measures, the church in contemporary American society is failing. Each year fewer people affiliate with the church and even fewer actively participate. While some would maintain that numbers cannot accurately reflect the quality of life in the church, it is our belief that the statistics, together with other indicators that we will discuss, are symptomatic of a malaise afflicting both church and society today. Individuals and institutions are searching for purpose, wholeness, and direction. The church has a stake in that search and a distinctive role to play in its successful completion; indeed, it is the church's search also.

At present some local churches are floundering. They have lost sight of their primary task. They are breaking all speed and activity records, but such activities have little effect because their objective is unclear. The result in many congregations is boredom or withdrawal by the members. The clergy become frustrated as the downward spiral continues; some leave the ministry, others busy themselves with activities that are only peripherally related to the church's primary task.

We do not believe that this situation is inevitable or hopeless. The church is an institution called into being by God, who works through it in individual communities to draw people to himself for healing. From the church he sends them out again renewed and strengthened for the task of leavening the part of the world in which they live.

This book is offered as a resource for ministers and congregations seeking a framework in which to think about the purpose and task of the church—one that will help them to synthesize their understanding of the Gospel on the one hand and the demands of their society on the other. It focuses on the demands made of the church by the people who continue to use it, the church's response to those demands, and the dilemma of those responsible for leading it.

The task we have set for ourselves is not a new one. Defining the purpose of the church, its distinctive function in society, and the task of ministry has received the attention of theologians and social scientists in every age. And that is as it should be—as society changes the church is changed. The task is never completed.

Nor can it be avoided. While we do not have to begin our effort from ground zero, we do have to start with a social milieu confronting humanity with concerns, conditions, and ambiguities never before experienced in exactly the same way. With some understanding of the sounds we hear around us, then, we may listen for God's Word, and seek to find that distinctive task and method that compels us to relate it and the social milieu.

The management of the church is not the primary focus of this book. It stands, rather, in the tradition of H. Richard Niebuhr's *The Purpose of the Church and Its Ministry*.[1] Niebuhr's book

---

[1] H. Richard Niebuhr. *The Purpose of the Church and Its Ministry* (New York: Harper and Row, 1956).

was based on a searching examination of theological education. He repeatedly drove home the point that the most important element missing in theological education was the integrating, unifying concept of the church necessary to pull together the highly enriched but disparate elements of seminary life. He saw clergy being equipped with sets of tools and procedures, but lacking the necessary unifying principles to remain daily aware of the purpose of the church and its ministry. Niebuhr was sharply critical of the assumption that church membership will automatically lead persons to an increased love of God and neighbor. Where the confusion prevails, "education necessarily becomes indoctrination in Christian principles rather than inquiry based on faith in God; or it is turned into training in methods for increasing the church rather than for guiding men to love God and neighbor."[2] We believe that a book that concentrates only on church management too easily contributes to the problem Niebuhr defined. This book is about the management of ministry, not just the management of an organization. We have striven for models of practice which integrate theological principles and behavioral action. We discuss church management and management principles because they are a piece of the life of the church, but only a piece to be integrated into the whole.

The purpose of this book is to help local church ministers understand their role and the role of the church and to manage its ministry more effectively. Ministers are the people in congregations who are called and set apart for a special role— leading and facilitating the body of Christ as it assembles for worship and nurture and disperses for service in the world. It has been our experience that the churches that have understood their essential task and discovered appropriate methods for implementing it are led by clergy who have a glimpse of what the church can be, and must be, and have provided a framework in which the congregation can function to make it so.

Lay people will find benefit here also. The book should help them to recognize more clearly the distinctive function of

---

[2]Ibid. p. 43.

the church in society and the church's ideal relationship to those areas of their lives lived outside of consecrated walls. If the book helps church members to sense for a fleeting second the power of people who have been redeemed, regenerated, and empowered as they are related to God, the congregations in which they participate will be changed and their individual lives will take on new meaning. This is not a devotional book. It is a serious attempt to help the church discover the power it possesses and effective channels for using it to transform the lives of individuals and communities.

Finally, we have kept in mind the needs of theological students who are hoping that they are giving their lives to an institution worthy of their loyalty; who, like their predecessors, are aware of the great personal and social needs in the world around them but are also disenchanted with the state of the church they have inherited and with the infrequency with which it addresses those needs; and who are searching for a system or frame of reference that will enable them to integrate masses of knowledge about church history, the Bible, theology, preaching, worship, pastoral care, and ethics in a way that will enable them to lead the church to renewal. The framework we are searching for may be a starting point. If so, our efforts are rewarded.

We have collaborated on all parts of this book over many months. Since the ideas of both of us are presented in every chapter, we have chosen not to state who is primarily responsible for writing each of the chapters. When an individual personal experience or encounter is related, it is the experience of one of us or a situation that one of us has knowledge of. In all cases we have changed the names and the details to protect the identities of the people involved.

A large number of people contributed to this volume, many of them unknowingly. They include the pastors and congregations who have invited us to participate in their lives, however briefly, as consultants and planners in recent years; our students at Intermet in Washington, D.C., and the Theological School of Drew University, who listened to and tested our early attempts to articulate our theories; and our colleagues in parish and congregational development who encouraged our efforts by listening and sharing their experiences with us.

James D. Anderson   Ezra Earl Jones
Washington, D.C.   *Dayton, Ohio*

1

The Dilemmas of Ministry

You are the pastor or an active lay person in a church in your community. Your relationship to the church is meaningful and important to you—most of the time. You glory in its strengths and fret about its weaknesses. Many of your friends participate in the church (your church or another one), but other friends have no church relationship. There are many things right about your church, many successes, but there are also aspects that are failing. On the one hand you recognize that the church is not dependent upon human efforts—"God is at work in the church"; on the other hand, you worry about problems in the church and feel responsibility for solving them.

You know the purpose of the church, yet when you are called upon to state it, the right words and concepts do not come easily. You often use the words *service, mission,* and *ministry* when speaking about the work of the church, but you can never define those words precisely; it depends on the specific situation. You feel that you participate in the church's ministry, but you sometimes wonder about the value of some of the things you do, or that the church does, and there is always the gnawing feeling that you ought to do more.

You recognize yourself as a leader in the church, for you do have many responsibilities, but it is often difficult to know what to do next and how to do it. You know your role as a leader is different from other group roles, but you are not sure just how. You believe in shared leadership, the priesthood of all believers, or group participation in decision making, but you are aware that "When everybody is in charge, nobody is in charge." What is a follower? What about members who neither lead nor follow?

Your church has programs for every age group, but new programs are always demanded. Some activities elicit widespread participation, others do not, and you are not sure of the reasons. The church organization appears to be adequately structured with boards, committees, and task groups, but not everyone understands the structure. Some people are always wanting to change it, and others hardly care. Some members are involved in everything; others barely make it to a worship service or special event once during the year. You wonder about the meaning of words such as *commitment, loyalty,* and *responsibility;* you are no longer sure about such terms as *salvation, discipleship, evangelism, holiness, heaven,* and *hell.* Too many people have too many different interpretations of these concepts.

The dichotomies and ambiguities of the church are real for you, but there is always someone or some event to challenge your carefully worked out synthesis. You can never get agreement on theological matters. Are people basically sinful or are they not? Is the church's basic task evangelism or social witness? Was Jesus God or the son of God? Are the bread and wine symbolic in The Lord's Supper or are they actually changed in the act of consecration? Can one be saved apart from the church? Is the "church" the building, the congregation, or a kind of mystical community?

You are aware that your church is located in and is part of a social setting (a community), but you are not sure what that means. You are vague in your own mind about the actual impact of the community on the church and of the church on the community. People often talk about that relationship (as do you) but seldom in specific terms. You know that most of the members of some churches live in the immediate neighborhood of the church, but that is not the case in your church, and it is difficult to know why that is. The community you lived in before this one was very different, and the church there was different too, but you are not sure about what made the churches different.

The three stories that follow are typical of the dilemmas of ministry. If you are a pastor, perhaps you can understand and emphathize with Bob, Joe, and Ted. If you are a lay person, maybe you know the feelings of their church members.

In 1966, following graduation from theological school, Bob became the pastor of a small congregation of 220 members, located three miles from a major industrial city. It was an area that had long been a farming community but was now beginning to develop slowly, with new homes in small subdivisions. Most of the new houses were between the church and the downtown area of the city, and few people other than the long-time residents of the area knew that the church existed. It was located one block off the main highway, hidden from view by an abandoned barn and a corn field.

Like many rural churches, this congregation was made up primarily of members of two large extended families. Fewer than 20 percent of the members were not related to one of these two families by birth or marriage. Traditions were strong in the church, and most of the members were not sure that the growth beginning to take place in their area was good for their community or their church.

During the first three months of his pastorate, Bob called on every family in the church. He learned about their lives, their concerns, and their previous involvement in church and community activities. As is usually the case, attendance during the first few months of his pastorate increased dramatically compared with the period just before he arrived.

By the end of the first year, twenty-three new members had joined the church, and only seven people had left. The budget was increased from $14,000 to $17,000, including a significant boost in benevolence giving. These accomplishments, together with the increased enthusiasm of the members, earned the congregation the "Church of the Year" award for the denomination in that region. From all observable signs Bob's ministry had been successful during his first year as pastor, and the future for him and the church was bright.

The second year had hardly begun, however, when imperfections began to appear in the life of the congregation. New members who had joined enthusiastically at first became inactive, and several families left the church before they had been members for even a year. Most were vague about their reasons for leaving but intimated that the church was not as open and progressive as they had thought at first. Long-time members of the congregation began to voice opposition to some changes in programs. An hour-long discussion by the official body of the church on whether the pastor was entitled to more than one week vacation each year led to hard feelings, and Bob recognized that progress and movement were not the goals of the majority of the church members as he had assumed.

Bob began to push the congregation to accept new outreach programs and to open the building to community groups needing a place to meet. He suggested a literacy program and support for a local mental-health clinic; these and other activities were rejected with little discussion. Attempts to redesign the Sunday school and provide a program of ongoing leadership training for teachers were also rebuffed.

By the end of Bob's third year in this parish, he could no longer tolerate the efforts of certain key people in the church to block his programs. He resigned the pastorate to become a personnel officer in industry in another state.

Bob did not have a framework adequate to make sense of the dilemmas he faced. He had personal ideals and goals regarding the potential of the church and assumed that his congregation could be led to share them. He had little sense of the congregation's understanding of the purpose of the church. His assumptions were not their assumptions; when that fact finally became apparent, it led to frustration for both pastor and congregation.

Joe is pastor of a neighborhood church in a city of 43,000 people. The church was once one of the largest of its denomination in the area, with more than 1,200 members. Today the church has 550 members and is declining slowly as older members die or move away and fewer neighborhood residents are affiliating with the congregation.

The church is located just outside the central business district in an area that was once the finest residential community in the city. The neighborhood has begun to change—some of the large stately houses have been redeveloped as professional offices or converted into multifamily apartments. Many of the houses in the area have been demolished and new apartment buildings erected.

Most of the members of the congregation today are over fifty years old, and many are over sixty-five. At one time more than 90 percent of the church's members lived within three miles of the church; few live in the immediate community today. The deterioration of the community and impending racial and social change has caused many former residents and their children to move to other areas of the city. While many of them continue to return to the church in their old neighborhood on Sunday, few are willing to come for evening activities, and every year several more families are lost to outlying churches.

Joe, now in his mid-fifties, has been pastor of this church for five years. He has watched the decaying condition of his congregation and the community around it during this period but has been helpless to slow the church's decline appreciably. He reports that the school immediately across the street from the church has become involved in many community programs for all ages and special-interest groups, which "has made it difficult for the church to find programs of a community nature it could do." Joe says that he has tried during the entire period of his pastorate to "get the church to serve the community," but that the congregation has never become enthusiastically supportive. He believes that if the church would build a gymnasium on the property behind the church, which could be done at a reasonable cost, it could compete with the school with recreational programs for the youth of the community and could again become an active institution.

Although Joe continues to prod the church to become more socially active, he has no illusions that such a "conservative group of people" will positively respond. He believes that it is his duty as a Christian to help meet human need wherever he finds it; he cannot be bound by a congregation that will not support him in his efforts. Therefore, he spends much of his own time in nonchurch community activities that the congregation will not support. Since Joe is a good preacher and is always present at committee and official meetings in the church, the congregation has not tried to dissuade him from pursuing his outside activities. However, some wish that he would spend more time in pastoral calling, particularly with the shut-ins, and a few people have expressed a need for more opportunities for prayer and Bible study in the church. Most members recognize, however, that Joe has little interest in such activities.

Joe had accepted the slogan that "a church should serve its community" without thinking through the type of service that a church is capable of rendering to its particular community. He gave no indication that he understood the congregation, the community, or the readiness of the congregation to serve a community that was no longer theirs. His training had not prepared him for translating theological values into the complex leadership decisions forced by a turbulent community setting.

Ted is a thirty-nine year old pastor of a church of seven hundred members in a suburb close to a large southwestern city. The church, only nineteen years old, is located in a fast developing residential neighborhood. In the three-and-a-half years of Ted's pastorate there, the church has registered a net growth of sixty-eight members. There are visitors at the worship services each Sunday morning, and few Sundays go by in which someone does not present himself or herself for membership.

The congregation is diverse. It is a family church but includes families of all ages. A large number of the adult members are in their thirties and forties, but there is also a large group over sixty. There are many junior and senior high youth in the church, although very few children between six and ten years old. The diversity of the membership calls for a wide range of programing in the church, including multiple worship and church school sessions, a strong women's group divided into eight units, a nursery school, a senior citizen's club, scout troops for boys and girls, and much more. A host of other organizations use the facilities during the week days. Numerous opportunities are offered to members and nonmembers alike for social involvement in community activities and social-action programs.

Ted is pleased with the progress the church has made during its history and particularly during his pastorate there. Although he is personally a well-organized administrator who keeps the scores of activities going in the church and manages to carry out his pastoral responsibilities with only a part-time assistant, Ted has come to realize in recent months that the long- and short-term goals of the church have never been articulated in such a way that overall direction is provided for the whole organization. He has come to feel that "the church runs him."

He has begun to ask questions. Why do people come to this church instead of other churches? Do the people find in this church what they need for their own religious pilgrimages? Does the local church have a distinctive task to fill that, in this church, is being left to chance while its many activities may or may not be related to that central task? How does a local church pastor lead a congregation to wrestle with these questions? As his fortieth birthday appraoches, Ted knows that he is a good leader and successful program developer, but he increasingly muses about the meaning of the merry-go-round of activity.

Bob, Joe, and Ted are not unlike the thousands of ministers of local congregations who deal every day with the questions of purpose, goals, strategies, and methods of ministry. They exemplify the men and women throughout Christendom who have heard and accepted the call to assume special roles within local churches. They are the people who have been trained to give leadership to one of society's primary social institutions, but who operate in roles that are complex and ambiguous.

To a large degree their role has been circumscribed for them. Their predecessors have initiated functions that are now theirs to carry out. Their congregations have particular expectations of them. In their own early local church experiences, in seminary, and now as ministers, they have learned the functions that have been ascribed to them and, for the most part, have internalized and assumed those roles for themselves.

The roles that accompany their chosen vocation present

them with a number of dilemmas. They are to be prophets, priests, and teachers. They have the responsibility of interpreting God's will for his people on the one hand and relating people in their sin and existential concerns to God on the other. They must challenge people to obedience at the same time that they comfort them in their afflictions. They must help people to rise above worldly concerns even as they lead them deeper into involvement with the immediate human needs around them. They must be cognizant of congregational and community traditions while initiating and supporting innovations in congregational activities. They must ensure that there are enough programs to serve the needs of their parish, and still be careful to preserve the quality and effectiveness of those programs. They must take seriously the pluralism and diversity of their constituency yet recognize that one of the primary tasks of the church is to help people find unity in the fragmentation of their lives.

Aware of the ideals for which the church was established, ministers are nevertheless daily confronted with the need for merely preserving the institution itself. They recognize that the church exists to extend itself outside of its own walls, but they must give attention to membership growth, finances, and building repairs.

They are sometimes caught between the demands of the denominational organization and the distinctive needs of the people who make up their congregations. They are reminded of their denominational responsibilities to serve as members of committees, boards, and agencies just when their own congregations are most in need of their time. The occasions when they seek to withdraw for study and renewal turn out to be times that the multiplicity of daily concerns within the parish are the greatest. They must constantly balance the need for efficiency in administration of the church with the necessity for delegating many tasks to volunteers who have little concept of the larger picture. As people in charge of organizations that cannot compel acceptance of organizational norms, they must determine the appropriate leadership stance in each situation and constantly shift from direct involvement in decision making to facilitating decision making by others.

They are managers whose first responsibility is to the congregations they serve, but who cannot limit their concern to the "insiders" who pay their salaries. They must be available to everyone in the congregation and the community at all times, yet they cannot have their time taken up with trivia and unimportant concerns.

They are people who must come to terms personally with the ambiguities of their roles as clergy on the one hand and as private citizens on the other—roles that are not always clearly defined and differentiated and that appear at times to be in conflict. As human beings they must deal with their own needs at the same time that they are confronted with the needs and concerns of others. The task of synthesizing the many demands of ministry is enormous. It would almost seem that the job of parish pastor is impossible for one person.

In the multiplicity of daily concerns related to conducting worship, providing Christian education, rendering pastoral care services, and administering the congregation, the parish minister needs a framework—a system—in which responsibilities and opportunities may be sorted out, priorities set, and activities related purposefully to other activities. If there is no framework at all, the best a person can do is give primary attention to some of the tasks (perhaps those he or she enjoys most), take care of other responsibilities when they become necessities, and let the rest go. If the framework is inadequate, the level of activity may be high but only "sound and fury, signifying nothing."

It is the pastor, then, who has to see through and go beyond the words of those who make demands of the church, to understand the real concerns of those who continue to be a part of it, and to enable those people, in the fellowship of the church, to find God's will. This does not mean that traditional forms and programs of the church will be discarded. It does mean, however, that every form and activity will be reassessed by each local congregation in light of its understanding of the purpose of the church, its primary task, and the needs and concerns of the people of the community in which the church is located.

The Task of the Congregation and the Role of the Pastor

The role of the pastor within the church is a crucial concern, which can only be understood in the context of the task of the congregation itself. The role of the pastor is different from the task of the church. In order to determine the distinctive role of the pastor, and in order for the pastor to construct a framework to enable the congregation to define its central task, the pastor and the church must first define why people go to church and the real demands that they make of it. In other words, the nature of the social institution determines the type of leadership and management that is needed. Failure to make the role of the parish minister relevant to the task of the church can only have one result: preoccupation with numerical success (in terms of either people or money). Examples abound of problems that have gone unsolved because of the way they have been stated or because of the lack of an integrated context in which to consider them.

During the past decade, most established Christian denominations in the United States lost members consistently every year. Denominational officials and local church leaders alike are concerned about this loss and have begun to look for means of reversing the decline. Suggested remedies include closing fewer churches, starting more new congregations, adding more programs in existing churches, making stronger visitation and recruitment efforts in local churches, and offering a greater variety of activities.

A high denominational official in a major Protestant denomination recently lamented at length the apathy in local congregations and proceeded to give five goals for every local church in his area. His goals were a net increase in attendance in every church, a net increase in church and church school membership in every church, training in Christian responsibility and stewardship in every church, full acceptance and payment of benevolence askings in every church, and giving to special mission projects by every church. He concluded by saying that if these goals were accepted and carried out, the membership decline would be stopped, and each local church would find new life.

This denominational leader, like most of us, responded to a problem in the church by seeking to remove the symptoms of the problem rather than by tackling the problem itself. At no time did he consider the reasons for the membership loss or the possibility that people were dropping out of the church because it no longer responded to their deep needs by relating their thirsting souls to God.

In the past few years we have frequently sat with groups of church people seeking to set goals for their churches for the following year. In almost every case the process was begun by group brainstorming about the needs of the church. With few exceptions, the resulting lists have been the same—needs usually include recruiting more people, raising more money, better training for leaders, better attendance at worship or church school, more and better activities for young people, construction of more or better facilities, and getting the congregation to be more concerned about community problems. In most cases the group then goes on to set goals on the basis of the stated needs. After the leader stresses that the goals should be specific, attainable, and measurable, the group generally aims to increase the membership by one new family per month, increase church school attendance by 10 percent, begin one new community project each quarter, or institute a certain number of new programs for the youth.

The problem with such needs and goals is that they are defined in institutional terms, completely separate from the task of the church and the personal needs of the church members and community residents. It is assumed that if more people participate in the church, more people will be served and served better. Often people within a local congregation discuss the merits of suggested changes quite apart from the real reasons changes may be needed. The person suggesting a change may not be clear why a change is needed and may, therefore, be able to go no further than to suggest that a problem exists. For example, church members who ask for more youth activities may be indicating that they are presently concerned about their own children—their moral values, their relationship to God, or their relationship to family and friends. Instituting additional youth activities may not be the proper response at all. Failure of the church, and particularly of the pastor, to recognize the background or context in which the suggestion is made may lead to discussing specific youth activities without first probing the nature of the need that has surfaced.

Another member may suggest that the congregation should be more socially involved. This person may actually be expressing his or her own need to be involved in the community but may not know how to pursue it independently. Perhaps it is easier to create new programs in the church and carry them out successfully than it is to set goals on the basis of the deeper needs of the people who make up the congregation.

Although the Christian church has lost influence in our society in recent years, millions of people continue to participate each week in local congregations in search of answers to the questions that arise in daily life. The real issue for the church today is whether it is concerned enough about those people to investigate the life situations out of which they come so that their questions may be adequately interpreted and their needs related to God in such a way that God becomes real for them. If this is the basic task of the church, then the problem for the parish minister is that of defining the intentions and providing the machinery and the facilitating environment that will allow the congregation to perform its task consistently and completely. An old man ran a variety store that at one time had been quite prosperous. During the man's later years, however, he spent all of his time arranging and rearranging the goods in his store but never unlocked the doors to receive customers. Having the merchandise well presented became more important than selling it. Many congregations operate at an institutional level much like this old man's store. The buildings may be in good repair, the people may be constantly cultivated and prepared for action, but little or no thought is given to the reason for the activity, and little activity occurs.

Such churches are not unlike the proverbial box, which, when the button on its side is pushed, opens its lid and reveals a hand that reaches out and closes the lid, turning the box off. Or they are like the coveted little toy that, in the words of the folk song, goes zip when it moves, pop when it stops, and whirr when it stands still, but, "Nobody ever knew just what it was, and I guess they never will."

The members of a Christian church may continue to come because of the potential that they see in the church or because of what they once experienced there. They may come because they enjoy helping to build strong organizations or being part of something that is big and successful. They may continue to come because of their historical ties with the institution. For some people attending church is assuring themselves of a place in heaven—a working out of their own salvation. It is as though they believe that God will have to admit into heaven those who have been loyal to an organization that calls itself a church. Some churches survive because there are enough of these people to keep the machine going. Traditional forms continue to have meaning for some people. There is always some benefit in the relationships that are established as people meet and work together. Most people prefer that weddings and funerals take place in the church. In some churches the worship services are the "best show" in town.

Unless a church moves beyond the point of being a successful organization, however, there will be a continuing subtle frustration for all participating. There will be a dropping away, and so a gradual decline in the membership of the church. The impact of God's revelation in the lives of individuals and societies will be reduced.

Perhaps it is the pastor who experiences the greatest frustration from attempting to manage a church that has only organizational goals. The pastor may be frustrated by an inability to understand the purpose of the church, by a congregation that demands institutional success (growth in membership, adequate financial resources, good buildings and equipment and many well-attended activities), or by denominational officials who require quantitative success. It is the pastor who is most harried by the demands of keeping a multifaceted organization functioning smoothly. It is the pastor who, every week, must meet the deadlines of sermons, worship services, outreach programs, bulletin preparation, building maintenance, and the like. It is the pastor who must be on constant call for emergencies and requests for special help from people in the church and the community. It is the pastor who always needs more time for sermon preparation, visitation, and program planning, and who suffers the most guilt when the time is not available. It is the pastor who has the most difficulty getting a firm grip on the job —setting personal goals and priorities that will help the members of the congregation to realize their goals. It is the pastor who has difficulty relating personal values and training to the purposes of the church and the Gospel. It is the pastor who is responsible to denominational administrators, who are also confused and overwhelmed by the task of managing congregations, and who must attend endless meetings to deal with the problem.

The pastor of a church in the Southeast recently wrote to the editor of a magazine for ministers. His letter was entitled "Frustration":

I have just come from a district church meeting. If it were my first it would not bother me. I might even be encouraged by it. But after twenty years I wonder.

By the end of the meeting I was not only tired but felt defeated. While I have no doubt that the church should be concerned about all human and spiritual needs, I wonder at times if we have a Messiah complex. Are we fooling ourselves to think the church can save the world? Maybe it can, but I'm not convinced that our planning and working will do it. We can't be everywhere all the time. We try to accomplish so much that we rarely see anything completed or even successfully done.

I also wonder if the structure of the church is such that any organization above the level of the local church thinks that nothing significant happens in the local church? Or that the local church is not at work in the world through its members where they live and work? A part of this comes from my frustration at never having enough time to plan, develop leadership or even do as much pastoral caring as I want to do because of meetings outside the local church. [1]

Is it possible for pastors of local churches to clarify their task sufficiently to be able to relate everyday demands to the

---

[1] Paul D. Lowder, "Frustration," *The Christian Ministry*, May 1975, p. 3.

essential task of ministry, to find direction for their own work and that of the congregation, and to develop a framework and methodology for accomplishing the task? How can pastors in their own planning and congregations in their functioning relate experiences in worship, nurture, outreach, fellowship, and administration in such a way that spiritual growth occurs in the lives of individuals and the communities served by the churches become more loving and just? Is it possible for all of these efforts to be integrated and put in perspective so that duties become opportunities rather than chores, and the task of managing the process becomes controllable? How is what takes place in worship related to the program of Christian education. How is the ministry carried out through funerals related to the ministry carried out through fellowship suppers in the congregation? In other words, how do most clergy understand the purpose of worship in today's church, and how appropriate is what happens there to the daily lives of the people who participate?

The pastor alone cannot enable congregations to define their purpose and then help them to define and reach their goals in relation to that purpose. As we have already indicated, the congregation has a stake and a responsibility in this problem; denominational leaders and agencies must also give attention to it. Is it not possible for those who hold responsibility for assisting pastors and congregations in their ministries to understand the "impossible" position of the pastor and begin efforts to develop new models and give support to pastors as they seek frameworks in which to operate? At the very least they can help to free them from institutional demands that tend to screen out the primary task of the church. Denominational personnel also must recognize the plight of congregations and the reasons for membership losses. They must help churches to rediscover the purpose that led people to seek out the church in an earlier time and assist congregations in adjusting to the societal change taking place around them. They can challenge congregations and clergy to move away from statistical measures of institutional success toward procedures that reflect the quality of lives redeemed, the fulfillment of human life, and the relation of people to God.

It is the contention of this book that the pastor's task is not inherently untenable. It is possible to get control, to see the larger perspective, and to fulfill the pastoral role without being controlled by it. To do this, however, the parish pastor must have a systematic frame of reference through which to minister to congregations in today's complex world.

We shall now turn our attention to defining ministry—the process by which people are related to God—and showing how the church and the pastor within the church may be effective in facilitating and sustaining that relationship. We will look at the components and the process of ministry in the context of a framework in which the task of ministry can be understood. The first half of this book is an explanation of the framework; the second half, beginning with Chapter 7, is devoted to application and example.

2

The Ministry System—Its Components and Process

There is a crucial difference between managing a church and managing ministry. The church is one critical component in a dynamic process of ministry that is primarily a relationship between people (as individuals and as members of society) and God's revelation (the Gospel). The pastor and lay leaders are set apart in the church for the key role of managing and facilitating that relationship. Ministry takes place within the church as people's needs are correlated with God's answers and as people who have been with God in the church are able to incorporate the divine revelation in the totality of their lives at home, work, and play. The church is an arena in which a *part* of the ministry process takes place. It is the setting in which people are related to God and prepared to enable other people to be related to God in the larger arena in which ministry occurs: the community. Ministry refers to relationships—people to God, people to people, church to community. One cannot talk about ministry without talking about both sides of the relationship. The minister who attempts to manage a church is already too narrowly limited and inevitably falls into preoccupation with institutional concerns.

The pastor of a declining inner-city congregation recently asked for "some models of successful urban parishes." The question reveals that this pastor's model of ministry is too small —it is so simplistic that it gets in the way of perceiving and responding to the realities of parish life. His own internal models of ministry do not allow him to ask explicit, external questions that bear enough on real life to be helpful. A model, after all, is always less complex than reality—the map is always less than the territory—but the models must capture enough of the essence to usefully represent real-life events and systems.

A broad view of ministry is needed. God's action in the world, the task of the church, the role of the Christian, and the role of the pastor within the church are all different from each other. Failure to recognize these differences puts the pastor in the impossible position of making the church, and primarily the pastor, God's agent in the world rather than supporters of people (church members) who are God's agents and are seeking to respond to God's love in Christ. What is needed in pastoral leadership today is trained people who can assist a congregation to think about its life, its faith commitments, its relations to the community, its care of its own members—help them think about the substance and quality of those commitments, and create the means whereby they can act upon them.

The concept described by the phrase *ministry of the church* always includes four components—community, reason for being, organization, and leadership. The relationship among these components is diagramed in Figure 1.

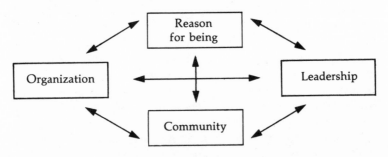

Figure 1. The Four Components of Ministry and Their Interrelationships.

This is simply to say that the urban pastor's request, if more appropriate or realistically phrased, would have addressed itself to the congregations' organizational forms and processes, the nature of their leadership, their reason for being, the shape of their communities, and the mutual relationships among these components. Moreover, the pastor's request for such information would be related to his understanding of this ministry system within his own situation.

The models we will present for each of the four components of the ministry system are fairly complex. They do not lend themselves to easy questions or answers. We believe that these models are richer, more adequate descriptions of parish life than are commonly utilized by church leaders. They are models that have borne the test of helping individuals see practical consequences and effect realistic action.

The Community

Any organization, regardless of its type, purpose, or size, exists in an environment over which it has some influence and which has some influence upon it. Some organizations exercise more power and control on the community in which they function than others, but few organizations have as much impact as they generally think they have. Taken together, the institutions and groups in a community may have a great deal of cumulative control, but there are additional outside forces over which local people may have little influence. The external forces and local controls together affect trends and events in the community that limit the power and importance of small-scale organizations and activities.

Regardless of the power an organization may have upon other groups or the total social context in which it operates, the setting of an organization—its community—always has tremendous influence upon it. Actually, terms such as *influence, control, power,* and *impact* are inappropriate in this regard. A social organization—a group of people banded together in enduring relationship for a particular purpose, through which people relate or carry out transactions—is part of the setting in which it exists. Participants in the organization are drawn from, yet continue as part of, the community.

In any community there are at least five primary social institutions, or basic social processes, in which people participate on a continuing basis—government, education, economics, family, and religion. Regardless of what they may be doing at any particular time, all people are citizens of their community, enjoying the safety and stability the government provides. They are related to the economic order through the giving and receiving of goods and services. Through schools and other structured educational processes, conversations, newspapers and magazines, and other communication media they are socialized for living in the community. They are members of families (perhaps single-person families) through which procreation is achieved and in which they find primary identification. All people in the community also work out, perhaps through religious institutions such as churches, a way to express their ultimate concerns and pursue answers to the questions of life's meaning.

All people, therefore, function through multiple relationships and roles, although they may seldom consciously differentiate among them. Everything that affects a person's life, from whatever source or role, affects that life in all of its relationships. Further, changes or activities in any one social institution or in the community generally affect all of the organizations in it. For example, the introduction of frozen foods clearly had a direct effect on the organization we call a grocery store. It also resulted in changes for all residents of the community by allowing more time for involvement in other institutions, giving more freedom to the person in the family who prepares meals, but requiring more money for the food budget.

A change in the family, such as the death of a father, may have an immediate economic impact. Another member of the family becomes head of the household. Participation in church and other voluntary organizations may change as the remaining family members become more or less active.

A community church is one organization in which some people participate. It is not the place where people practice their religion—that is a continuous process that occurs wherever they are; it is where they work it out, develop it and seek to understand it. What goes on in the church building ideally affects the total lives of the members and, beyond that, the lives of people they touch. Conversely, what goes on in the church is influenced by the character of the community it serves. To be precise, at times during the week a part of the community moves into the church (which is itself in the community) for a purpose that is related to the life of the community. The first basic component in the system of ministry, then, is the community in which a church exists and in which it was initiated and designed.

In this book we use the word community primarily to indicate a geographical area, the area around a local church. It may be a small residential neighborhood, a part of a city, or an entire metropolitan area. Some special case churches serve people distributed sparsely over a fairly large geographical area through a distinctive or unique ministry. For these special-case churches community is used with a secondary meaning: the people who attend and support the church and are a part of its ministry.

The Reason for Being

There is a reason for the existence of any community organization: It makes some contribution to the social life of the community. A business or group is not formed merely because someone decides to start it, or one or more people decide that more groups or organizations are needed. At the core of the organization is an idea, a need, a coalescing principle that brings people together. The proprietor of the grocery store sets up business to provide food for the community and to earn a living. A group of people organize an investment club in order to pool their resources and skills to obtain additional assets. A civic club comes into being as a group of people share a common commitment to meet a certain need or relate to one another in a particular way. A hospital is built in the community not because every community must have one but to offer health care.

A church is established because a group of people who share a common religious heritage or denominational affiliation have a desire to work out their religious faith and offer their ministry to the community. The reason for being—the understanding and execution of mission—is the second basic component of ministry.

The Organization

The third necessary component of ministry is the organization which gives it primary support. In order to fulfill its purpose, a group of people establishes a structure. Every group must have an operational process, facilities and equipment; schedules, norms, and values; or other organizational characteristics in order to function. A family generally has a building of some type in which most family life takes place. In addition, there are schedules of sleeping, eating, bathing, watching television, and so on that are generally accepted by all family members. In all likelihood there will be a division of labor whereby individual family members carry out certain functions for the good of the family as a whole. A hospital requires a building, beds, attendants, schedules of visiting hours, specialized equipment for various procedures, and so on, in order to fulfill its purpose of rendering health care to the community. In a similar fashion, a church requires some form of organizational structure to fulfill its mission and purpose in the community.

Leadership

The fourth basic component of ministry is its leadership. A leaderless group cannot endure. Leadership may be shared within a group, it may change from time to time, it may be democratic or autocratic, but it must be effectively and continuously performed if the organization is to fulfill its purpose and survive. A hospital could not operate without an administrator and doctors who manage the health care of patients. A construction firm without management would only by chance approach a construction project with adequate workers, plans, raw materials, and tools.

A church, although it is a voluntary organization, similarly designates people to direct the total activities of the organization. Like other institutions, the church could not operate without leadership.

Leaders and managers are the people or groups responsible for articulating the direction of the organization at a particular time in its existence, or facilitating the group's doing it. This entails knowing, understanding, and incorporating changes taking place in the environment, and structuring the organization so that it may fulfill its task. The manager of the organization may perform certain tasks personally and delegate others. Regardless of the intangible nature of much of the church's organizational work, it is someone's responsibility to see that it is done efficiently, at the proper time, and in an appropriate relationship to other tasks that are required.

The Process of Ministry

For ministry to function at an optimal level, all four components must be correlated. The process of ministry breaks down when any one of the four components of ministry is overlooked or subordinated to the others. The ministry also breaks down when forms and processes intended for relating people to God through the church are severed or become dysfunctional for any reason. Because of the importance of these relationships and the four components themselves, we discuss them further in succeeding chapters.

People in a community organize a local church for a purpose. They share common religious traditions and have needs and concerns with which they believe the church can help them. Some come often; others only occasionally. Some find a place of service in the fellowship of the church; others do not tarry long in the church but perform their ministries to others through nonchurch involvements. Some come to the church in brokenness, in grief, or unhappiness; others come to give expression and witness to the goodness and love they have experienced.

For whatever reason and in whatever social-psychological state, they come to be related to God. As they come into the fellowship of the congregation, they may be renewed and transformed. In the liturgy, in Bible study, in sharing with people like themselves who are also searching, they may find God. As they return to their daily lives as family members, citizens, workers, students, and the like, they carry with them what they have found in the church. As they leave the church, they have been strengthened. They do not leave God or spiritual things behind—they go out and God goes with them.

They have been redeemed and changed, and as they participate in the world, they bring redemption and rebirth to those whose lives they touch. The church becomes manifest in the community in their lives. The church changes and influences society through the people who live there and work there.

The ministry of the church can no longer be seen as the management of a congregation. It is not recruiting members, raising money, preaching sermons, conducting Sunday school classes, or scheduling activities, although all of these processes may be required. Ministry is the process of interrelating the four components we have discussed. It is the congregation as an organization, led by one or more managers, receiving people, relating them to God, and preparing them to live their lives as whole people in their communities.

The ministry of the church, therefore, has two focuses—first, those who participate in it as members of the congregation; and second, the people, processes, and structures of society that are touched by the members of the congregation in the community. The end of the church's efforts is to enable its members, through a foundation of Christian faith, to create a society where all people are loved and are loving, where justice and compassion characterize relationships. It is on this basis, and not just on the basis of the church's institutional health, that the success of the church's ministry can be evaluated.

The church is not the only institution that works to such a purpose; other social institutions and organizations may pursue that goal also. The task of the church, however, is unique. It alone is charged with the responsibility of helping to bring about more just and loving relationships in all institutions and social involvements through correlating people with God, the source and ground of their being, through relating the creature to the Creator, the weak with the source of all strength.

The pastor's role in the process of ministry is an enabling one. It is not his or her ministry—ministry belongs to the whole congregation—nor his or her responsibility to do the ministry—all members carry out the ministry. The pastor's role is to minister to the ministers and to be a catalyst in the church—one who causes and facilitates the process of ministry but who is not personally "used up" by it. A catalyst, by definition, participates in a process of transformation and facilitates its occurrence, but it is not itself changed or harmed in any way by the process. In the church, when the role of the congregation and the role of the pastor is confused, so that the pastor assumes the responsibilities of the congregation, ministry does not occur and the pastor becomes frustrated, harried, and ineffective. The ministry is to those who come to the church to be related to God. It is the pastor's job to manage their coming and their going out. The church's ministry is performed by those who come and then return to society to serve.

In order for pastors to perform their role effectively, they must be knowledgeable about and conversant with the community served by the church; understand the nature of religious quests and the faith of the church historically regarding God's activity in the world; have some knowledge about the structures, forms, and processes that enable the church to perform its role in ministry; and understand their own abilities, weaknesses, and personality and how they affect the performance of their duties.

3

The Local Church and Its Community

On June 30, 1977, a church died in Springfield. A scant twenty-five years before, it was the largest Congregational church in New England and the fifth largest Congregational church in the United States. Located on Winchester Square in Springfield, Massachusetts, once a fashionable residential area, Hope Church "fell victim to the flux of population shifting from urban to suburban, and from white to black."[1]

Hope Church was organized in 1876, although a mission had been started as early as 1865.

"Hope flourished during the early part of the 20th century, floundered a bit during the depression, then . . . reached its pinnacle over the next 20 years. By 1952, membership reached 2,837, the largest of any Congregational Church in New England. . . .

Like many churches, Hope Church became swept up in the churning rapids of societal change. Yet it was like flotsam caught in a swirling eddy and pushed to a stagnant backwater. The price it and others like it pay for their detachment from the community is disbandment; and for its members, as well as for the entire community, it is the most severe and wrenching price of all."

Hope Church is one more in a long procession of major protestant congregations (several score in 1977) that have closed or will close. They are located in communities experiencing radical and basic change. The churches cannot accommo-

---

[1]Stephen Altshuler, "Death of a Church," *Yankee*, April, 1977, pp. 92–108. All quotations pertaining to Hope Church are from this source.

date the change; hence, they decline. When a church's self-identity is at odds with the character of the community, and when that situation endures for several years, the only alternative for the church is eventual death. Two other churches, St. Peter's Episcopal Church and Wesley Methodist Church, located in the same community, have been more successful. "St. Peter's represents a rare example of a fully integrated church: 60% Black, 40% White, with a White priest. They are mostly working people, living in the Winchester Square area and sharing a strong religious experience. . . . Wesley Methodist Church, next door to Hope had been predominantly White until about five years ago. At that time a number of members from a fragmented Black church joined Wesley and most of their White members left. It is now 85% Black. . . ."

The members of Hope Church could not have prevented the change from taking place in their community, nor is it reasonable to assume that the membership of the church would not dwindle during this period. The community changed, and the new people had no stake in the church. Hope Church was not responsible for the change in the community, but is responsible for the way it reacted to the change. It is there that we may wish things had been different.

The Context of Community

Ministry always takes place in a setting—a community. It is in the context of the community, a geographical area with multiple social institutions and complex relationships, that people live their lives and are related to God and other people.

People may change the social context in which they live by moving from one community to another, or the community itself may change. But during a specified period of time, a particular community is the arena in which people participate in family relationships, go to school, earn a living, establish friendships, pay taxes, elect governmental officials to serve them, and participate in civic clubs, recreational and entertainment events, and church activities.

The primary community for most people is the geographical neighborhood in which their home is located. In addition to sleeping and eating most meals there, many other relationships and activities are generally based there. It is often the area where adults vote, children go to school, the whole family shops, and where important one-to-one relationships are developed. It is also possible to define community in nongeographical ways. People may define their community as the group of people with whom they work or socialize, or relate to in other important ways. The larger group may be drawn from many geographical areas. This is often the case for people who live in nontraditional family units, such as students, single people of all ages, or childless couples. How ever people define them, communities are settings where people find identity and grounding for their lives, where personalities are formed and aspirations developed in intimate relationships. Communities are where values are grounded and the context in which major lifetime decisions are made.

Churches exist in and reflect the character of their communities. It sounds simplistic; it is almost a tautology; but it must be said again and again until we, the members of churches, understand that simple phrase better than we do now. A church cannot exist for long apart from a community. It is an institution created within the community to fulfill a special function for the community. A local church is a segment of the community celebrating or practicing its common faith; a church that loses its community loses its life. When a congregation begins to see itself as having an identity apart from the identity of the community as preceived by the people who live there, that congregation is moving toward its inevitable demise. A church with a preponderance of members living outside the community in which it is located has already passed being a community social institution and has lost its reason for being. This is not to say that all congregations die as their communities change. But it is true that in order to live through and beyond community change, intentional awareness and adjustment are necessary.

Normally a church grows and develops as the community is growing. During the community's years of stability, the church remains stable. When the community begins to decline, it is normal and natural for the church to decline with it. Some churches change as their communities change, perhaps declining to dangerously low levels, although they remain a part of the geographical community. These churches are generally able to maintain their lives. Other churches remain a part of the community as long as the community is stable. But if the church tries to hold to what the community used to be when the community begins to change, ultimately the changing community will pass it by. The church that gets out of step with its community is in the most danger of limiting or even losing its ministry. This was the predicament of Hope Church in Springfield.

It has been our experience that in the early years of their existence, most churches pay close attention to the important relationship between community and congregation and congregational programing. It is not uncommon, however, for churches in their later years to become "closed systems," which lose sight of the environment in which they exist. In this case, the churches tend to set goals and make decisions only on the basis of internal information.

If the task of the church is to receive people in their need and relate them to God, the church must understand the life situations of the people who come. The church must be knowledgeable about the people and the community structures and processes that produced their present concerns. It must understand people as individuals, as families, as classes, as races, as workers, as political parties. It must know their self-sufficiencies and handicaps, their strengths and weaknesses, their likes and dislikes, their opportunities and limitations, their joys and sorrows, their hurts and exultations. And it must be aware of changes in these characteristics as they occur over time.

Perhaps understanding the community served by a local church is the most difficult and time-consuming responsibility that the pastor and congregation have. Since the social setting is always changing, the job is never done. As times goes on and the pace of change accelerates, the task becomes even more difficult. Of course the church must interpret and act on the information as it is gathered. Understanding is only the first step in the process of ministry, but it is basic to all of the others.

One local church pastor pointed out the urgency of understanding the constituency in a parable:

The waiting room was filled to capacity and people were standing along the wall. All ages were represented. Their ailments were as varied as the names. The doctor came out and instructed the nurse to give everyone two tablespoons of castor oil, a shot of penicillin, and a bottle of vitamin pills. No, the above did not happen. The doctor dealt with each patient individually, listening to a description of his ailment and prescribing treatment accordingly.

The shoe shop was filled with customers. Some had big feet and some had small feet. Some had high insteps and some had flat feet. Some feet were narrow and some were wide. The salesman came in with an armload of men's oxfords, black, size 8, and proceeded to put them on everyone in the room. No, that didn't happen either. He measured each foot in turn, asked about styles preferred, and fitted everyone accordingly.

The waitress looked out at the tables filled with hungry diners. There were fat ones, skinny ones, short ones, and tall ones. She turned to the serving window and shouted to the cook, "Corned beef hash for everyone." No, that wasn't the way it was. She took a menu around and each one ordered according to his taste and appetite.

In the pews the worshippers waited. They were young and old, male and female, married, single, separated, divorced, healthy, sick, weak, strong, possessors of doctoral degrees, and high school dropouts. Some were glad and some were sad. Some were friends, and some were strangers. Some were rich and some were poor. Some were confident and some were worried. The preacher entered the pulpit and spoke to them saying. . . .[2]

Defining the Church's Community

Just as people may define their basic community in different ways, churches also use differing criteria in defining their communities. Frequently churches find that, after several years, members of the congregation move to other communities yet continue to come back to the former community for church activities. There is thus a temptation for church leaders to define the church's community in terms of the people who

---

[2]Martin Pikes, as quoted in *First Christian Church News*, Alice, Texas, vol. III, no. 22, June 5, 1975, p. 1.

make up its membership and attend its functions rather than in terms of the geographical area in which it is located and in which most of the people lived when they first made contact with the church. How a church defines its community determines how the church will act or react—thus whether it will live or die—when the community begins to change. If the church understands its community as the people in the geographical area where it is located, it will generally attempt to change as the people who inhabit the area change. In this case it may continue to serve in that place. On the other hand, if the church thinks of "its people" simply as its own members, it will probably consider relocating to another geographical area when its members begin to move in significant numbers to other neighborhoods, or it will attempt to continue without change where it is.

Every church has a community or parish area for which it has responsibility—often sole responsibility. It is imperative that each church realistically define the boundaries of the geographical area or the special characteristics of the people it presently serves or can serve. But as we have seen, the total area encompassing the residences of members often cannot be defined as the church's community. A congregation's parish— its community—is that neighborhood, cluster of neighborhoods, or group of people attracted because of the church's distinctive style or task, in which the church can reach out to new people and attract them into the congregation. In general, people choose a church that they believe is related to the other involvements of their lives, that they feel to be a part of their basic community, and that helps them to integrate their lives.

Since people relate to their environment in different ways, they differ in their perceptions of their communities. Some prefer a church that reaches out to or offers them the possibility of involvement in the whole city, the whole metropolitan area, or a large part of the county in which they live. Others relate primarily to only one neighborhood, or perhaps to a cluster of neighborhoods. For still others the primary community is the ethnic, racial, language, religious, or interest group with which they identify.

There are essentially six types of churches based on the

scope of the community they serve or have the possibility of serving. We describe them here as a framework in which congregations may appropriately define their communities.

1. A neighborhood church is located in a fairly well-defined and contained residential area. In many ways it is clearly identified with the neighborhood and may share its name with the community. The church may be somewhat hidden on a side street or secondary road through the area rather than on the primary street leading into the city. The community will generally be relatively homogeneous in terms of cost and type of housing, race, and social class. If this is not true currently, it is because the community has begun to change. In all likelihood, the church was organized in the early stages of development of the community, grew as the community developed, and remained relatively stable until the community began to change, if that point has been reached. If the community is more than a few years old, a number of members have moved out of the community, but few people have ever joined this church who did not live in or have close ties to the community itself. The future of the neighborhood church is intimately tied to the character of the residential area immediately surrounding it—indeed, that is its community. As long as there are people in the neighborhood and the church actively serves and recruits them, the church can continue. The church cannot survive except as it adjusts to community changes. When the neighborhood church defines its community by its members rather than by the neighborhood, it has taken the first step toward the loss of its ministry.

2. A metropolitan regional church serves a large part of the metropolis or region in which it is located, but rarely the entire inhabited area. It has a visible and accessible location that enables it to be identified with a larger part of the urban area than is true of a neighborhood church. It is strategically located on a major thoroughfare leading out of the center-city area. It was organized as the city began to grow in that direction. Its community may well be a large slice of a city, including both urban and suburban neighborhoods. The area is often one of middle- to upper-middle-class homes—the "in" place to live, at least when the area was first developed. The metropolitan regional

church usually grows rapidly and becomes quite large. Because of its size and the character of the community it serves, this type of church may well be the status church of its denomination in the area.

3. Churches located in the downtown central business districts of cities are unique in their ability to reach out to all areas of the city and suburbs to serve people and attract members. Although few people will go to another part of the city or a residential neighborhood that does not have some relationship to their own to attend church, many people want to participate in the life of the whole city and so choose to participate in a church at its center. The downtown church is likely the oldest church of its denomination in the city. It has been and may continue to be large and prestigious. It likely has had a wider range of social classes in its membership than any other type of church because of its ability to reach into all types of neighborhoods. The community of the downtown church, therefore, is not merely the downtown or inner-city area. It is that and much, much more—the whole city and often the entire metropolitan area.

4. The communities of special-purpose churches are not defined by geography. A special-purpose church is one that attracts people because of its unique theology, distinctive style of ministry, or other exceptional quality. The special-purpose church may be quite small or very large, depending on the number of people who want a church that is distinctive in this particular way and upon the quality of its program. The entire life of a special-purpose church is different from other churches in the area and other churches of its denomination. The community of the special-purpose church is defined as the people, whoever they are and wherever they live, who react positively to its special appeal. The church may be located anywhere, as members may drive long distances to participate.

5. A church located in a small town of several hundred to several thousand population typically serves the people living in the sparsely populated area surrounding the town as well as the immediate townspeople. It is the only church of its denomination in the town. It may be similar to a downtown church in its history and diversity, but its organization, programing, and

patterns of relationships resemble those of the neighborhood church. The community of the small-town church, then, is the town and its surrounding areas.

6. The open-country church located at a crossroads or on a secondary highway in a rural area serves the sparsely populated region surrounding it. Its community may overlap with the service area (community) of the small-town church. It is typically small in membership and building size, slow to change, and noticeably populated by one or more extended families. The program offerings of the open-country church are simple and traditional—weekly or biweekly worship services, a Sunday school, a women's group, an occasional church business meeting, and perhaps a youth group. As in a neighborhood church, participants may include former residents of the area who have now moved to a nearby town or city but return for church activities.

As a result of community change or deliberate decisions by church members and leaders, a church may change from one type to another. A downtown church may become a special purpose church, often limiting the scope of its outreach. A metropolitan regional church, following a radical transition in the area in which the church is located, may find it difficult to serve or recruit new members outside of its immediate neighborhood, and it becomes essentially a neighborhood church. The most common change occurs when a small-town or open-country area evolves into a suburb of a larger nearby city. The churches may take on the character of neighborhood or metropolitan regional congregations. Frequently churches that are uncertain about their task and future direction are in just this situation—moving from one type to another. As the transition occurs, some members perceive the church according to its former type; others envision a new and different type of congregation.

It is imperative that churches accurately define the scope of their communities. As we have seen, however, it is not a decision that a congregation makes on the basis of where it wants to serve or recruit members. It is a definition based upon the sociological realities of where the church can serve and serve well. The downtown church that limits its concern to the inner city will not survive as an institution and will miss important opportunities for ministry. On the other hand, the neighborhood church that tries to minister to the whole city, or to other neighborhoods within the city, dissipates its energies and resources and thereby fails to adequately serve the area for which it does have responsibility.

Social Characteristics of the Community—Trends and Processes

A major difficulty in understanding the community served by a local church is the volatility of social trends and processes. Changes take place so rapidly that trends are relegated to history before they are adequately understood. The impact of social change on the church and the community vary according to a number of factors, including the openness with which people accept change, the nature and depth of the change (whether it is basic to the fabric of society or superficial, with only limited effects), and its permanence (some changes being only temporary and having only short-term effect). The difficulty in determining the impact of a change, however, does not justify failure to discriminate.

Societal processes with significant influence upon the church vary according to the scope and scale of their penetration. Some processes are worldwide while others effect only the nation or a part of it. Other trends, although perhaps quite powerful, may be limited to one or a few cities.

At any given time in a given community there may be scores of social trends and processes at work that have important consequences for social relationships, for the quality of life in the community, and for the ministry of the church. The larger the community, the more complex are the processes at work. Following are some examples of the range of social processes and how they work in a community:

1. Systems and networks. Operating in the community may be street gangs, the school system, denominational and ecumenical coalitions, political parties, the chamber of commerce, labor unions, a narcotics ring, and a public utility authority.

2. Power blocks and lobbies. The Democratic Party and labor unions may team up in an upcoming election against a Republican challenger for mayor. The Citizens for Better Schools may organize to get the Board of Education to construct a gymnasium. A coalition of contractors, architects, and real estate agents may join ranks to pressure the local zoning board for variances to build apartments in an exclusive part of the city. A group of irate citizens on the Flood Control Committee may ask for tax relief in the wake of severe flooding in their section of town.

3. Issues and problems. Winners in the next election will probably be those candidates who convince the citizens that they can do the best job in lowering taxes, providing housing for senior citizens, constructing the new community swimming pool withot an increase in taxes, eliminating the drug problem in the senior high school, and getting the county to complete the widening of the major thoroughfare through the town. In addition, citizens may be worried about inflation, snow removal, the opening of some stores on Sunday, parking in the downtown area, and an increase in the number of nonwhite residents in the town.

4. Status and class differences. There are rich and poor, educated and uneducated, laborers and business executives, "blue bloods" and newcomers. Some people let their property deteriorate while others spend lavishly to keep their homes well maintained. Some buy groceries with food stamps; others eat most of their meals at the exclusive country club.

5. Accepted norms, values, and morality codes. For some the traditional norms still hold; for others men are no longer expected to give their seats to women on public transportation, and divorce is thought to be superior to unhappy marriages. Premarital sex may be the norm rather than the exception among college-age students, but cohabitation by unmarried people of opposite sexes is still frowned upon. Homosexuality is anathema.

6. Institutions, agencies, and organizations. There are civic clubs, schools, hospitals, rest homes, a college, a center for the physically handicapped, churches, retail and wholesale businesses, an industrial park, a fraternal lodge, and a senior citizens' club.

7. A community ethos. For most of the people of the community, the dominant feeling at this time is one of frustration and distrust of government, of concern for middle-class values, of increasing conservatism in politics and support of charities, and a longing for the good old days. At another time the "sense" of the community may be very different.

The attributes of the hypothetical community we have delineated, and many, many more that could be mentioned, singly and in combination, have both short- and long-range consequences for the people who live in the community, positive for some and detrimental for others. The fact that such processes affect human life and human relationships, however, means that they underlie the needs, concerns, and life situations of those people in the community who call upon the church. If the church is to be successful in responding to needs and accepting people with an understanding of their deeper yearnings, it must understand the community trends and processes that influenced them. The local congregation must be specific in analyzing how the church is directly and indirectly affected—how it usually responds to this knowledge, and how it should respond. That task is not an optional one for the local church; without it the ministry is irrelevant.

Stages in the Life Cycle of a Community

Communities, like people, are not static. They are dynamic and changing, growing older and getting younger. Often the later stages in a community's existence are similar to early ones. Neighborhoods go through stages that parallel the life cycle of the majority of their residents. When occupied by younger families, the neighborhood is teeming and thriving. As the population ages and the children grow up and leave, the community tends to lose its vigor. Later, as the older people sell property to a new group of younger families, the community may again take on new vitality. The circulation of housing and people is an unending process of life. The buildings themselves go through a normal aging process; as they get older, they require more maintenance, and some of the original equipment requires replacement.

It is our contention that God does not call the local parish church to survive, but to attach its life to the lives of the people in the community that it has the possibility of serving. At whatever stage in its life cycle a community may be, the church, in order to serve it optimally, must be at that same stage in its existence. When the community is growing, the church should be growing. When the community is dying, the church should be dying. The death of the old community and the old church makes possible the building of a new neighborhood and a new parish church to serve it. Without the death, there can be no resurrection. Today we often find churches struggling to maintain stability in the face of community change and decline. It is a losing battle; it is inappropriate.

There are five basic stages through which communities move, which a local church should be able to identify. There are newly developing communities, stable communities, pretransitional communities, communities in transition, and post-transitional communities (those that have changed and are again stable). A church's life should follow the same cycle. Those churches that understand the phase through which their communities are passing are the churches which will serve them well.

We shall look briefly at each stage of community life and its typical characteristics:

1. *The newly developing community.* This is an area of open land or a sparsely populated area in which new dwelling units are constructed over a period of several years. The residential growth may be very rapid, with most of the area being developed in only a year or so, or it may take up to a generation (twenty-five to thirty years) for the area to become fully developed. Most such developing communities are 90 percent completed within a few years. In most cases the houses are in the middle-to upper-middle-class range. There is also some development of commercial properties and social institutions. Some businesses will be established very early. Social institutions, such as schools, clubs, and churches, are organized as the number of residents increases. Basic services for the community are developed over the entire period, and there are few social problems during this stage of the community's life.

2. *Stable communities.* The longest stage in the community's existence will generally be the period of stability, which may last up to several centuries. Some communities however, begin to change almost as soon as they are fully developed. Most communities enjoy a period of stability from thirty to seventy years in length. During this period the community is made up of a homogeneous population with a normal distribution of age groups—a large number of families with school-age children and proportionately fewer elderly people. At this stage of the community's existence, there is little construction of buildings, basic services and social institutions are intact, there are few social problems, and there is high involvement in neighborhood activities and groups.

3. *Pretransitional communities.* "A pre-transitional neighborhood is one where the conditions for change are present, but minorities (people with basically different characteristics than the original residents) have not yet entered, or one in which they are present but not in sufficient numbers to disturb the balance of the housing market."[3] The pretransitional period may last a decade or more but generally covers a period of only a few years. One begins to notice an older population and fewer children. The school population begins to stabilize or decline, the demand for housing shrinks, there are more deaths in the community, houses stay on the market longer, and involvement in neighborhood institutions and activities slows. In the older neighborhoods adjacent to this community, communities are already well along into the transitional period.

Stability is primarily a function of housing supply and demand. "A racially mixed neighborhood can be maintained in the long run only if there is sufficient housing demand from both whites and minorities. If the only demand for housing is from minority persons, that community has already entered the transitional period." In the pretransitional communities, there-

---

[3]James H. Davis and Woodie White, "Patterns of Pluralism," unpublished paper circulated privately. Davis and White are clergymen who have studied churches in racially changing communities. Subsequent quotations pertaining to stages of community development are from this source.

fore, demand for housing by people with the same characteristics as the majority of the population continues, but that demand is noticeably slackening.

Just to look at an area, it may be difficult to distinguish a pretransitional neighborhood from one that is stable but slightly hetereogeneous in its ethnic, age, or life-style mix. For this reason few people are aware that a community is changing until the change is well along.

4. *Communities in transition.* This is the stage in the community's life that may endure for a generation, but more often lasts a decade or less. It is the stage when the majority becomes aware of the presence of minority people, or people who are different than they are in some way, and begin to act upon that recognition. Different people act at different times, and they may take different actions. Similarly, various neighborhoods respond differently. If the community is in racial transition, the original group (generally the whites) will become increasingly aware of the presence of the new group and more and more of them will move away.

The primary characteristics of a community in transition are rapid turnover of property and an increase in the amount of rental property; the presence of more children and older people, with few in their middle years; an increase in social problems and conflict; widespread deterioration of property and an increase in the rate of sale of property; decreases in involvement in neighborhood institutions, often to the point where many close; increasing participation in community institutions by people who now live outside the community; the development of new local institutions; a heterogeneous population; and the construction of some new buildings, primarily commercial or apartment complexes in the place of deteriorated housing.

"Looking at the community as a whole, there seems to be a 'tipping point' where the community is no longer stable racially. The housing market becomes unstable because a sufficient number of former residents have decided that the community is being (or will become) dominantly a minority community and they no longer want to live there." At this point the community begins to change rapidly from the former group to the new group.

A rule of thumb is that when a community becomes 25

percent minority and the neighborhood school is approximately 40 percent minority, the community is at the tipping point. At that time the quality of municipal services begins to deteriorate, the rate of social change is at its highest, and disorganization is at its greatest.

5. *Posttransitional communities.* The posttransitional stage, often a new period of stability, occurs when the new group of residents becomes the numerical majority in the community. The community power shifts, and the newcomers begin to participate in decisions affecting their community. The posttransitional community is essentially a new community. "Sociologically, it is just as new as a suburban subdivision, but its newness is less obvious because the housing is not newly constructed. In the suburbs the people and the houses are new. In the transitional communities only the people are new." Although the posttransitional community may last for several generations, it generally has some stability for a score or more years. Again the community is basically homogeneous. The age distribution of the population is again relatively balanced, with a large number of school-age children in the neighborhood. There is little construction during this period. Basic services and institutions are intact, although perhaps at a lower level than before. There are fewer outside controlled institutions, and local involvement in neighborhood institutions increases. "Like other new communities, the post-transitional community has an excitement, vigor, and status. For awhile, it is the 'in' place to live, to have a business, to move your church," at least for the new residents.

It is our contention that churches that recognize when their communities are in the pretransitional period and plan appropriately for their futures are those that can move through the transitional period to the new stability of the posttransitional period as viable institutions. These are the churches that can take on new life as part of the new community. On the other hand, churches that do not act until the transitional period is well along ultimately die, relocate, or find some other less than acceptable alternative. These are the congregations that suffer most.

The transitional period in a community's life is not unlike the time the community was being developed originally. Further, the posttransitional period is not unlike the longer, happier period of stability the first residents enjoyed. If church people and all citizens could come to see that a changing community is not dying but is being re-created, and could treat it and its social institutions as new opportunities rather than problems, there would be less discomfort in changing communities, and the chances for successful new communities and new institutions would be greatly enhanced.

Stability has always played an important role in the development of social institutions, including the church. People who live stable and consistent lives, including employment and a sense of permanance, are more open to participation in a church or community group. We cannot expect stable churches to persist through unstable times while communities are changing. They must participate in the instability of the moment in order to participate in the coming stability of the posttransitional period.

Churches are part of and serve the communities in which they are located. Regrettably, religious institutions sometimes tend to take on lives of their own apart from their communities. This danger is heightened at the time the community is moving into the pretransitional and transitional stages of its existence. People who are different economically, culturally, racially, religiously, and in other ways, become threats, and long-time residents begin to escape or draw into their own circle, lock their doors, and shut out the new people.

When a church loses touch with the people in its community, the community has lost the one institution that can help people understand what is happening to them and the one that can challenge them to open up all of their relationships to include a wider circle. When the church itself becomes exclusive, refuses to reach out to the new people, and begins to think of its life as a social institution apart from the community, there is no longer that caring, life-giving institution that can help the whole community to adjust. There is then no possibility for the church to make its primary contribution to the community at the time it is needed the most.

4

Ministry and the Structure
of the Local Church

The Issue of Organization and Structure

"Concern for the structures of the church, and particularly for the need of changing them is . . . not to be understood only as social adjustment to changing conditions but also as an expression of obedience to God's mission."[1]We spent several hours some months ago in the company of a key leader of one of the major Protestant denominations. This denomination was in the throes of a full-scale effort to restructure and reorganize. So massive and unsettling was the restructure that it had become the major topic of conversation for the leadership of the communion. The first five minutes of business phone calls were inevitably consumed by a recitation of the "woes engendered by the restructure." The denominational executive, in commenting on the situation, went into great detail concerning the lack of theological, historical, and sociological thought and analysis behind the changes being made. Of course, we were speaking to only one individual about a change national in scope and enormous in consequences, but the conversation had great impact on us. We were forced to face once again how easily the institutional church ignores examining the fundamental sources of its orders and structures in its attempt to coexist in the hurly-burly complexity of today's world. The

---

[1] *The Church for Others and the Church for the World, A Quest for Structures for Missionary Congregations* (Geneva: World Council of Churches, 1967). All quotations and references to the World Council of Churches are from this source.

church talks theology but is managed expediently. Legislated structural change, divorced from an integral clarification of the mission of the church, is a fiasco we can no longer afford.

Every pastor of a congregation is the chief executive officer of an organizational structure that constitutes the primary environment of church membership. At the same time, the pastor is a member of a sacred association of baptized persons—a part of the priesthood of all believers. There are no simple models for the structure of the church.

As the church historian Robert Paul has pointed out, the classic manner the church has chosen to answer the question, "What form of the church expresses the will of Christ?" is in terms of polity.[2] This is simply to say that our Christian ancestors had the conviction that there is a functional relationship between the form the church takes and the Gospel it intends to proclaim. We are not eager to return to an era of ecclesiological debate over the respective validity of episcopal, congregational, or presbyterian forms of polity. We do want to point out that it is an ancient Christian tradition to assert the authority of the church's structure as a mediation of the authority of Jesus Christ. To subscribe to this principle does not mean that we must believe that there is present in the New Testament and in church tradition a form of church structure immutably preordained for all time. The restoration of church structure to its New Testament purity is an empty literalism. At the same time, the spirit behind this recurrent theme in our history is essential to our health. It is the belief that ecclesiastical forms can facilitate or hinder the transmission of the essential Gospel message in a particular time and place. From the point of view of a student of organizational life, it is to take with the utmost seriousness the power of social structure to shape our destiny as human beings.

From time to time this important emphasis upon organizational elements surfaces in a renewed search for the "best" or most effective form of church life. Thus the World Council of Churches in 1967 published the results of a four year study on

---

[2] Robert Paul, *The Church in Search of Itself* (Grand Rapids, Mich.: Eerdmans, 1972).

the missionary structure of the congregation. The study was an attempt to examine the practical implications for structure of the mission of the church in a new world. It took seriously the disappearance in western society of the small, isolated, rural communities where the parish had once been the effective missionary structure. It was the premise of this World Council study that new structures were needed in this new age if the church was to "confront life at its most significant points." A recent series of commentaries printed in the World Council of Churches' "Monthly Letter About Evangelism" noted that, while the original 1967 study helped to spawn projects such as industrial missions and urban training centers (which were funded by the traditional structures), what it did not do was to change the missionary structure of the local congregation.[3]In the 1970's the programs, processes, and shape of the local congregation are once again undergoing examination. The social mission imperative of the '60s has disappeared. In a document of enormous political importance for middle American Protestantism, Dean Kelley set the direction for this inquiry. His argument that the reason for the decline of the liberal Protestant churches is their lack of strictness in matters of faith and belief, and hence a kind of lukewarm relativism in the membership, has become a permanent backdrop to the present-day mission and structure debate.[4]The enormous numerical growth of the neo-Pentecostal movement and the continued relative decline of the "mainline Protestant" bodies have combined to keep the spotlight on mission as evangelism, and evangelism as church growth. Numerous denominational studies have been spawned dissecting local church programs and policies and attempting to uncover the differences between those churches that are growing and those that are declining. New and renewed interest is being shown in the work of the Institute of Church Growth at Fuller Seminary in Pasadena, California. The

---

[3]"The Missionary Structure of the Congregation. An Unfinished Task." *A Monthly Letter About Evangelism.* No. 10, 11, 12. Oct., Nov., Dec. 1975.
[4]Dean Kelley, *Why Conservative Churches Are Growing.* (New York: Harper and Row, 1972).

denominational studies and the books and conferences of the Institute represent persuasive and influential forces on the thinking of church leaders about the structure of the local congregation. We will use some of these studies as illustrative material in developing our own model of the local congregation. We do so because the studies are contemporary and because the questions they address are so often the questions church people are currently asking. Nevertheless, while the trend of the church in the '70s seems to be away from the liberal answers reflected in the social involvement structures of the '60s, this should not blind us to the fact that the theological and practical questions under debate remain the same: What is the will of Christ for the church? And what form of the church expresses that will?

What do we mean by church structure?

Organization, or structure, is one of the four components of the system of ministry. Managing a congregation is not the equivalent of the management of ministry; the organizational arrangements of a church are but one aspect of the total ministry system. Nevertheless, it is a rare list of a local church's problems that doesn't contain such issues as:

Are we properly organized?

Many committees exist in name only and seldom function; what are we doing wrong?

The youth group doesn't function the way it used to; it doesn't have momentum.

Such questions have found their focus in recent years in the issue of membership growth and decline: "Is there a way to organize a youth group and get more young people involved?"

This chapter is a guide to the elements of the structure of congregational life. We will examine the nature of these elements and the ways the total structure must fit with the particular church's leaders, the execution of its mission, and the characteristics of its community. As in the other sections of this book, we assert that a self-conscious model is necessary if we are to avoid a mindless round of organizational restructuring.

Traditional concepts of organization structure follow the typical printed organization chart, which specifies formal relationships and describes degrees of authority and positions. For many people such a chart has been their only means of analyzing and understanding an organization. Thus in the 1967 World Council of Churches study subtitled *A Quest for Structures for Missionary Congregations,* we assume structure meant "organizational model." From several points of view the word *structure* is a misleading term for the total concept of a church as an organized, regularized entity. Structure is, however, the common church word, and no other word as readily points to the general area of concern.

In a conversation with a prominant church executive we casually mentioned that he should be aware that the local church is a more complex body to understand than a single human being. To our astonishment the official was surprised by the statement. His own concept of organization was that of a static blueprint. The only complexity his organizational model could contain was increasing the number of lines and boxes on the chart. Just as a doctor must understand the human body, so such leaders must be able to understand the organized body we call the local church. One would be unhappy with a doctor who could only draw pictures of the shape of the body and who had little knowledge or awareness of the unseen anatomy and the many systemic aspects of the physiological and psychological functioning.

"Organized body" is perhaps the best synonym for the element of the ministry system we have labeled organization or structure. We mean both the anatomy and the physiology of the church. We are referring to all of those formal and informal, visible and invisible, organized, enduring elements, processes and programs of that body we call the local church.

The primary unit of any social system is an individual human being. Our capacity as human beings (what we are made for) far transcends any work assignments we might be given. Unlike a machine built to perform one simple function, we are capable of a vast range of functions. Assigned to write an article, we may choose to daydream or write a book. As a family we periodically redesign the formal organizational structure by which the weekly household chores will be accomplished. An analysis of the family subsystem for household maintenance would reveal that a constantly shifting set of dynamics and multiple functions are involved that have nothing to do with dishwashing, carpet sweeping, and lawn mowing. Our formal rules for household maintenance are often less influential and persistent than the informal ways we work together. Some people like to think of the formal structure of an organization as the piece of the iceberg that shows above the water. The largest part of an iceberg is the reality underwater. It is this invisible but major portion of the iceberg that is analogous to the informal, functional side of our church organizational model. Any structure made up of human beings will function in a variety of persistent patterns that transcend the formal structural design. So important is this basic reality that it can be well argued that "a social system is a structuring of events or happenings rather than of physical parts and it therefore has no structure apart from its functioning."[5]

Practically speaking, this is to say that when the questions arise—What is wrong with this organization? Why is the church not growing? What's wrong with the missionary structure of the congregation?—the analysis and redesign must clearly examine the functional interrelationships among persons and groups, the actual dynamics of church life, not just an organization chart of boxes and lines. A group organized for fellowship may actually function as a center for spite and gossip.

An understanding of the structure of the system of ministry must include both the anatomy and physiology of church life. We must be interested in the overt ways we divide up the work and the covert ways we work together. Hans Kung reminds us that the word *ecclesia* means both the process of assembling together and the concrete assembly itself.[6] The church

---

[5]Daniel Katz and Robert L. Kahn, *The Social Psychology of Organizations* (New York: Wiley, 1967).
[6]Hans Kung, *On Being a Christian* (New York: Doubleday, 1976).

exists as assembly because of the constantly renewed process of assembling.

A second important distinction is between an association and a bureaucracy. The fundamental nature of the church is that of an association. We are a group of people who have voluntarily associated in common cause. The nature of an association flows from the common goals of its members. The leaders of an association work for the membership in order to help them move together toward the common goal. This associative, voluntary principle is at the heart of the church in the United States. The reality, even for the Roman Catholic Church, is that congregations form around a voluntary decision to belong to the church of choice not merely on the basis of geographical boundaries. Most denominations have chosen to allow the congregation to select their ordained leaders. Those denominations that place their clergy by executive order still find that the minister must work through a covert process of authentication by the membership.

An association is a flat organization—members are equal in status. In contrast, a bureaucracy is "a stratified employment heirarchy with at least one manager who has a staff of employed subordinates."[7] The members of a bureaucracy work for the boss, who is generally called a manager. Once again, notice the contrast with the leader of an association, in which the membership as a whole constitutes the "boss."

As the sociologist, Elliot Jaques, has pointed out, associations are the creators of bureaucracies. Associations form stratified bureaucracies with managers and employees as they are needed for the association to accomplish its ends. The church is no exception. Each denomination has created its own set of regional and national bureaucratic agencies. These agencies have managers and several levels of employees.

Thus our experience of the church is of both an association and a bureaucracy. This is true even at the level of the local church. Every local congregation has some elements of bureau-

---

[7]Elliott Jaques, *A General Theory of Bureaucracy* (New York: Halsted Press, 1976).

cratic organization in its life. It may hire a small staff of secretaries, maintenance personnel, and program staff specialists. From this point of view the chief minister is the manager of a small, bureaucratic organization. Even though these tasks are being performed by volunteers, the same boss–subordinate quality may still pertain. People will become employees for payoff other than money. There is a set of administrative jobs that bear no intrinsic relationship to the goal of the church but must be performed if the fabric is to be maintained. As soon as a congregation is financially able, these tasks are naturally structured into a small bureaucratic organization that the minister must manage. In some large congregations a business manager is hired to handle these matters.

Employees can be held accountable; volunteers cannot. However, the members of a volunteer association can be supportive to one another. Leadership in a voluntary society can provide guidance and can confront irresponsible behavior.

The church is a comingled association and bureaucracy. The necessity to distinguish between the two and to focus upon the essential, associational nature of the church is basic to our discussion of the structure of ministry.

Church leaders must reckon with the fact that the single most important reality of organizational design is that there is no one best way to organize in all situations. Organizational structure must be both comprehensive and situational. Buying an organizational model off the rack is always a mistake. The contingency approach means that the manager of church structure must learn to be a tailor. The primary management task is to alter the continuing processes and structures of church life to the specific situation. Like a good tailor the manager of church structure has to be able to measure the present situation, assess the fit, and perform the necessary alterations. The continuing search for the best way to organize for the surefire new program is one of the worst and most common mistakes of church leaders.

The varied shapes of the local church require a multiplicity of fabrics, patterns, and stitches. The issue of organization "fit" will recur again and again in this chapter. In particular, note the way in which the fit between the church and the community it serves is a prime determinant of the shape of the local church.

As an example, we cite the Church of the Resurrection in Alexandria, Virginia, which serves a highly transient community of highrise apartments and townhouses. Election to the church board is by a lottery in which the names of prospective new board members are drawn out of a hat. The role requirements of board membership have been carefully spelled out so that those selected are given an honorable option of accepting or declining their chance selection. The method works admirably. Time and again individuals who have been in the congregation less than a year have been selected, have accepted, and have served well. This way of organizing a church election isn't the best for everyone. It is, however, a good fit for this congregation in its community of diversity and transiency.

This contingency approach to the missionary structure of the congregation is well illustrated by a lengthy study of membership growth and decline in United Presbyterian congregations. We summarize the study in the next section of this chapter. The list of factors studied in and of itself is a good indicator of the complex set of programs, processes, elements and units which go together to make up the anatomy and physiology of the organized body we call the local church.

Member Growth and Congregational Models

"Membership Trends in the United Presbyterian Church"[8] is a study of more than six hundred congregations categorized by growth and decline in membership. The report is rich in statistical data and summary findings. It does ask the reader to assume that numerical growth is positive and that it can be an indicator of effective and faithful ministry. We believe that this is an important relationship, and that much can be learned from the study of the organizational model of an effective mission congregation. At the same time, however, we believe that the final test of a congregation's effectiveness lies not in how many

---

[8]"Membership Trends in the United Presbyterian Church in the U.S.A." Research Report—Special Committee of the General Assembly Mission Council, 1976; source of all references to and summaries of the study.

people enter but in what they take with them as they go back out into society.

The study does not tell us as much as we might hope about the informal functioning of the congregation. It tells us clearly the members' perception of such issues as leadership, influence, decision processes, and member motivation. While this is useful information, it is not the picture of actual functioning that would emerge from observation and interview. The study is primarily a comparison of the characteristics of growing congregations, declining congregations, and congregations which were stable or had declined slightly.

We have summarized the findings of the study in the comparisons in Tables A–C.

TABLE A
Satisfactions and dissatisfactions in growing and declining congregations

Growing congregations characterized by:	Declining congregations characterized by:
Most satisfaction with: Preaching Worship Pastor Programs Congregational openness to new ideas Methods of organization Sense of mutual encouragement, support, and homogeneity Member motivation	Lowest satisfaction with all of these elements of parish life
Least dissatisfaction with congregation's involvement in social issues	Tendency to blame social involvement for membership decline
A program emphasis on spiritual growth, Christian education, and youth	A program emphasis on fellowship, worship, planning, with least emphasis on youth
Adequate procedures for incorporating new members, including formal membership class	Few or no procedures for educating and incorporating new members
Congregational involvement in member recruitment	Little participation in new member recruitment
Affirmation of Bible in faith and practice	Affirmation of Bible in faith and practice

Growing congregations characterized by:	Declining congregations characterized by:
Little felt need for membership growth	Eagerness for new members
Members' affirmation and participation in secular, voluntary organizations	Tendency to see participation in secular organizations as a barrier to church involvement
High degree of identification with surrounding community and culture	Feeling separate, alienated from culture, community life styles

TABLE B
Important statistical and demographic differences between growing and declining congregations

Growing congregations more likely to be:	Declining congregations more likely to be:
Younger	Composed of a higher percentage of people sixty-five and older
Wealthier	Composed of greater percentage of retired people
Located in a suburb with newer, owner-occupied housing	Located in neighborhoods with a higher percentage of single adults and aged people living in older, rented housing
Drawing members from wider geographical area	Located in racially changing neighborhoods
Located in community with an increasing school population	Receiving new members who differ in race, economics, class, age from longer term members
Further away from other Protestant congregations	

TABLE C
Factors and forces that seemingly do not distinguish growing and declining congregations

Degree of social involvement
Use of many, varied devices for communication
Percentage of small-group involvement
Stringency of membership requirements
Sharing of faith with others
Approach to moral issues
Style of worship
Overall theological conservatism or liberalism
Degree of identification with or satisfaction with the denomination, synod, and presbytery worship
Perception of levels of coordination and influence
Degree of follow-up on inactive members

There is some good news and some bad news for church leaders in this study. Among the good news is the fact that even at a time when a denomination is experiencing an overall decline in numbers, many congregations continue to increase their numbers. Good news for some and bad news for others is the fact that there is no single explanation for growth and decline —both societal and institutional forces are involved. The nature, range, intensity, and interrelationship of these forces, whether we are speaking of the American church as a whole, a single denomination, or a solitary congregation, defies reduction to a single factor. It may be bad news to many that pat formulas and canned programs (under any title) will not build a congregation. The good news is that there is a lengthy and practical list of actions that can be derived from the findings. The study is a means of helping us to examine the forms of church structure and the relationship of structure to the other elements of the ministry system.

The Structure of Ministry

The relationship between structure and community

Being indigenous—identification with the community.   The single most important factor shaping congregational structure should be appropriateness to the nature of the surrounding community. The Presbyterian study highlights again and again the fact that "the community in which a congregation is located usually makes a significant difference as to the potential for growth or decline." No matter how hard a congregation works, its environment may determine its fate. Church leaders are conditioned to assume that any and all changes in the environment can be accomodated by adjustments within the existing organization. This is manifestly untrue, and yet countless clergy feel guilty and depressed about the state of the congregation they serve because they assume that if the preaching were better, the program more exciting, and the congregation more friendly, then the dilemmas posed by a changing community and neighborhood could be resolved by the existing congregation. Notice

in Table A that growing congregations had an identity with
their community; that is, members felt an identification with
the values and life style of the community. They saw no barrier
to parish participation from active participation in other community affairs. Their actual demographic profile was more similar to the profile of the community than that in declining congregations: 48 percent felt to a great extent a part of the church
neighborhood as contrasted to 38 percent in declining congregations.

Donald McGavran provides supporting evidence in his
book *Understanding Church Growth,*[9] which has grown out of the
theologically conservative, sound scholarship and research of
the Institute of Church Growth. Utilizing historical analysis as
well as the tools of the social sciences, the Institute has investigated the causes of church growth in different cultures and in
different historical periods. Their findings, without using the
terminology, continually reflect the reality of a good fit between
community and structure. Among reasons for growth McGavran cites:

*Someone had a particular plan for multiplying churches which fitted his special
population;*
*Environmental and church factors favorable to growth appeared at the same
time;*
Indigenous leaders and indigenous church principles were utilized.

A mission will not grow if it is alien or foreign to the culture
in which it finds itself. Successful business enterprises that rely
on sales and marketing programs are simply attempting to manage the transactions between the enterprise and its environment. Through technological invention and service competence, or by marketing activities, the enterprise alters and
expands the demands that consumer groups are liable to make
upon it. A truly missionary model of the congregation would
focus on the degree to which the parish is alien to or indigenous
to the culture and community in which it finds itself.

---

[9]Donald McGavran, *Understanding Church Growth* (Grand Rapids, Mich.:
Eerdmans, 1970). References to McGaveran's findings are based on this
source.

Not too long ago the search committee of a small, rural, Southern congregation talked of the things they liked and disliked in the previous pastor and of their hopes for a future leader. A favorite story told with obvious pleasure and enthusiasm was of the expastor's attempt to grow a vegetable garden on the grounds of the parsonage. Every family present had a similar garden next to their own home. In contrast they wished to avoid calling a pastor whose interests would lead to involvement in the activities and interests of the nearest urban center. Too often they had experienced pastors who, like visitors from a foreign land, brought strange customs, refused to learn theirs, and soon moved back to their own land. Effective ministry calls for indigenous structure.

The melting pot concept of community.   McGavran's advice for evangelizing urban populations includes the dictum to "multiply tribe, caste and language churches". This may seem strange advice to an institution accustomed to melting pot images of community:

Here there cannot be Greek and Jew, Circumcised and uncircumcised, barbarian, Sythian, slave, free man, but Christ is all, and in all (Col. 3:11, RSV).

But what is possible for the church as a whole may be impossible for an individual congregation. Moreover, every local community of Christians must live in the tension of the fellowship that by the grace of God it has already become, and the vision of the Kingdom not yet realized. Conversion and transformation are continuous processes.

In 1962 Gibson Winter gave just the opposite advice and recommended the establishment of sector congregations.[10] Winter quite clearly noted the lack of challenge in the comfortable suburban ghetto. To overcome the ghetto isolation of the suburbs, Winter prescribed the establishment of congregations that slice diagonally through an urban area so as to emphasize true economic and racial diversity. As Urban Holmes, the dean

---

[10]Gibson Winter, *The Suburban Captivity of the Churches* (New York: Macmillan, 1962).

of Sewanee Seminary, has recently noted, this was impossible advice. "It is the homogeneous, small, natural community from which the ecclesia emerges. This is necessary for the life of a community whose vocation is from God not from the city planning board."[11]

The Presbyterian membership study provides additional evidence that diversity is a serious impediment to the growth of fellowship and membership. Pious hope and pulpit rhetoric do not change human nature, especially when it comes to our capacity to live with difference. Seventy-eight percent of the rapidly declining Presbyterian congregations were in changing communities. Twenty-six percent of the growing congregations indicated that new members were different from long-term members, whereas 46 percent of slightly declining parishes and over 50 percent of the rapidly declining congregations noted such differences in members.

We have had occasion to observe a number of declining congregations which adopted the tactic of combining their worship services. Reasons given for this action included a wish for a greater sense of community, the discouragement caused by sparsely attended services, and the general economics of money and energy. The predictable outcome of such a decision is to accelerate membership decline. Within two years the single service has lapsed to the attendance figure it had before combining occurred, and any trace of the other services is gone. We believe that it is important to understand the theoretical and functional reasons for these failures.

Professors Paul Lawrence and Jay Lorsch of Harvard University have provided the theory and research needed to make sense of these phenomena.[12] Their basic research stemmed from the comparative study of six organizations, all operating in the same industrial environment. They have stated that an incentive for their work was their perception that most organizational research and theory had focused on "the one best way to

[11]Urban T. Holmes, III, *Ministry and Imagination* (New York: Seabury, 1976).
[12]Paul R. Lawrence and Jay W. Lorsch, *Organization and Environment* (Homewood: Irwin, 1967).

organize in all situations." It was their belief that a much more fruitful avenue was in seeking the answer to the kind of organization it takes to deal with a variety of environmental conditions. Their criticism is certainly applicable to most discussions of the missionary structure (model) of the congregation, and their reformation strikes at the center of declining congregation difficulties uncovered in the Presbyterian study.

Lawrence and Lorsch utilized the concept of differentiation and integration as their theoretical formulation. As systems grow larger, they differentiate into parts that must be integrated for the effective functioning of the whole. As a congregation grows, it may differentiate its organization, creating, for example, a "super-sixties" group and a "young couples" group, which must then be integrated into the life of the congregation as a whole. The segmentation of an organization is a part of its adaptation to the environment. Sales departments relate to customers, while production must be concerned with the suppliers of new materials.

Lawrence and Lorsch focused on the problem of different external environmental conditions requiring different organizational characteristics and behavioral patterns in order to be a successful enterprise. They further assumed that organizations well designed for the demands of their external environment would create high levels of motivation for the members by providing them with settings in which they could do their individual jobs well. Four attitudes of each subgroup were measured in order to assess differentiation:

1. Members' orientation toward goals—to what extent members in different groups used different goal criteria in decision making.

2. Time orientation of members—long or short time-span orientation.

3. Interpersonal orientation—orientation toward task or toward social relationships.

4. Formality of structure—measured by characteristics such as the importance of formal rules, span of control, specificity of performance criteria, and hierarchical levels.

To measure differing external environments Lawerence and Lorsch developed a concept of certain and uncertain environments. This was measured by judgments with regard to:

1. Clarity of information from the environment.

2. Degree of uncertainty in cause and effect relationships.

3. Time span of definitive feedback.

Thus an environment could be characterized as stable or certain if it provided clear information, certainty in causal relationships and rapid feedback of data.

Thinking about these variables with regard to communities in transition and pretransition is instructive. A pretransition community is difficult to identify. It can be years before one can be sure that a decline in the church school is due to an aging community rather than an ineffective program. As a community moves into transition, apartments appear with restricted access and high turnover. Community participation declines and so does the consequent flow of information regarding community trends and needs. Transition and pre-transition communities are uncertain environments. There is a high degree of uncertainity in cause and effect relationships. Clear, valid information regarding the community is difficult to obtain. Timely feedback on the impact of new programs can be totally absent.

The findings of Lawrence and Lorsch can be briefly summarized. First, the companies with highest performance in an uncertain environment were those displaying the greatest differentiation and integration. Great intellectual and emotional differences were discovered among the managers of subunits in these companies. At the same time the most effective organizations had developed integrative devices that assured effective collaboration between departments. A second discovery was that differentiation and integration are essentially antagonistic states. The Presbyterian study found that the constructive handling of congregational conflict was a more important determinant of growth than the degree of controversial social involvement. Lawrence and Lorsch note that in an organization in which different groups have different goals, norms, and orientations—which must be true if the organization is to effectively cope with an uncertain environment—then intergroup conflict is an inevitable part of organizational life.

Drawing together what we have learned so far, and returning to the example of declining congregations combining worship services, an explanation begins to emerge. We know that a declining congregation is likely to be serving a changing neighborhood or community—a turbulent environment. The decision to combine services is a decision to decrease the degree of differentiation. Instead of offering new members two or three different times to attend and a range of available styles of worship they must be content with the single option now open to them. Because the new members probably differ in values or life stage from the longer term members they are likely to be seeking a different set of worship activities. The task of assimilating new members is not the same task as nurturing stable members. The combined service creates increased opportunities for intergroup conflict within the existing congregation by placing together groups with differing orientations and values. Latent intergroup conflict, which in the past was managed largely by organizational separation, may now become unexpectedly manifest.[13]

Lawrence and Lorsch discovered differences within one company that were too subtle to be easily visible, even to those who belonged; so the presence and importance of difference are often invisible to church leaders and members. Thus a new mission to the Hispanic community in a large metropolitan center may fail to grow in members because its structure does not recognize the differences in the various nationalities comprising the total Hispanic population. Recent studies done by Warren J. Hartman in the United Methodist Church clearly identified five different "audiences" among the membership of the United Methodist Church:[14]

---

[13]See Richard E. Walton, "Third Party Roles in Interdepartmental Conflict," *Industrial Relations,* October 1967, vol. 7, no 1, for a summary of ways to modify organizational structure to reduce conflict potential.
[14]Warren J. Hartman, *Membership Trends: A Study of Decline and Growth in the United Methodist Church 1949—1975* (Nashville, Tenn.: Discipleship Resources, 1976).

1. *Fellowship group.* Individuals looking for affiliation and support. A highly mobile, well-educated group. Contains young and old, and a large number of men.

2. *Evangelistic concerns group.* An extremely loyal group who are concerned to win others to Christ and the church. The oldest group with the lowest education and income levels in the United Methodist study.

3. *Study group.* A young, highly educated group supplying a disproportionate share of leadership. They seek opportunities for involvement and education.

4. *Social concerns group.* A small group with a high percentage of women. This group is eager to involve the church in community and world issues. It is the group with the poorest record of church attendance.

5. *The mixed bag group.* Individuals who share two or more of the above concerns, often fellowship coupled with one of the other areas.

Each of these groups differed significantly regarding the satisfactions they were seeking and the values they were expressing in their desire to join and participate. The integration of each grouping into the life of a congregation demands a conscious differentiation of program and activity keyed to their differing values and expectations. The greater the number and size of such audiences in any one local church the more difficult becomes the process of differentiation and integration, and the higher the potential for conflict. If the community to which the congregation must turn its evangelistic effort is characterized by strong, diverse groupings, then congregational structure becomes quite complicated. The more differences in the congregation and the community, the more uncertainty there is about the congregation's task; hence a vastly increased need for information, leading to increased strain on the congregation's communication processes and a loss of interdependence and integration. The more turbulent the situation, the more information must be processed, and the greater the chance for confusion and fruitless conflict. Congregations in pretransition and transition communities must structure to handle a wide variety of groups.

They need to build increased communication processes and learn how to manage difference in ways that retain a sense of community.

Congregations frequently develop adult education programs by looking for a single educational offering appropriate to the entire membership. This approach works well only if the congregation is all of one age bracket, sex, and life style. Adults seek education which is instrumental to the resolution of their particular goals and concerns. These issues are highly varied as affected by stage of life, values, socio-economic status, sex, and situation. Note the length and variety of adult education courses typically offered by such community agencies as the YMCA, city recreation department, and local college extension program. One agency's recent brochure had over twenty courses ranging from philosophy to weaving. Among the courses listed were offerings in auto mechanics, meditation, parent effectiveness training, and financial investment.

For many congregations it only takes offering one additional course to double the choice presented to the members. By contrasting styles of teaching as well as course content, members can be given the chance to select a program more suited to their own unique situation. A small group discussion of divorced and widowed persons and a lecture series on the Old Testament prophets present these contrasts in style, format, and content. Homogeneous congregations in a stable community can get by with offering a single adult program and urging all members to attend in the name of unity and communal fellowship. As the community changes and diverse groups begin to appear, the church must learn to offer more options. Congregational at-one-ness must then take other forms than the solidarity of attendance at a single educational event. The strengths of the fit between individual need and congregational program response can become part of the new cohesive glue of church life.

All of this is not to say that there are not congregations capable of handling such diversity and uncertainty, but that they are clearly the exception and not the rule. To achieve enough communication for the adequate integration of diverse individuals and groups is a difficult and continuous task. The structures and processes of congregational life must be capable of producing a deep sense of belonging and community in order even to have the opportunity to speak of the Gospel to the great bulk of seeking people.

Structuring a place to belong

A recent meeting of Christian educators, asked to select their own model of the church, chose as the dominant form of ministry the development of the church as a living form of community. The church as family is a common goal of congregational life. The organization or structure of a congregation is intimately related to the issues of membership, belonging, and fellowship. At its center a church is an ecological environment: It is groups and individuals living in an interdependent balance with one another. Words and phrases like organizational climate, environment, and social setting are used to emphasize the fragile ecology of human community, which, like a mountain meadow, is dependent on the subtle interplay of the forces of setting, climate, and individual beings.

The goodness of the fit between individual and congregation Hartman's study of membership trends in the United Methodist Church concludes that "church growth may be more closely related to a sense of acceptance by a warm, supportive Christian community than by any other factor." The dominant factor in the choice of a local church by over two thirds of 1657 people Hartman surveyed was "friendliness of the people." The Presbyterian study emphasized the presence of congregational involvement in membership recruitment and well-executed procedures for incorporating new members through membership courses as distinguishing marks of a growing congregation.

Carl Dudley, in a study of small Presbyterian congregations,[15] states that their strength, as measured by per-capita attendance and financial giving, is significantly higher than

---

[15]Carl S. Dudley, *Unique Dynamics of the Small Church* (Washington, D. C.: The Alban Institute, 1977).

larger congregations. He attributed this to the fact that small congregations derive their unique strength from being a "single cell," a close network of caring people. The small parish is the right size for people to know each other personally and to achieve the deeply shared sense of being a loving community. "Like the primary family group, the small church offers intimacy and security of people who can be trusted, even with silence."

If Dudley is right about the strength of the small church, why do the "experts" on the small church today write books about and counsel us to save the small church and expand its outreach by gathering it up with other small churches in larger parishes, group ministries, and other variations of church clusters. The trend is to try to make small congregations like big ones—more resources, more people involved in programs, and more energy expended on structuring, planning, and organizing. The lay people of small congregations rarely seek these coalescing structures on their own. The ideal of cooperation sounds good, and so far few people have been able to articulate the inherent fallacy in the idea. The problem is that we are concerned to help the small church "do things," when its strength lies in what it is—a primary group of caring people.

The implication of Dudley's research for large churches is that successful larger congregations would be built of multiple cells, each of which is the community of concern for its members. This concept is not new, of course, and is well stated by C. Peter Wagner of the Institute of Church Growth.[16] Wagner's conclusion is that effective growing churches combine celebrative worship with a deep sense of community. The community is created by two different-size building blocks—congregation and cell. He defines congregation as the fellowship of the up to two hundred members one might be expected to know by acquaintance and name. In a statement of the need for differentiation and integration, Wagner suggests that as a church grows beyond that number, it should create additional adult congregations (fellowship groups of up to two hundred members), and

---

[16]C. Peter Wagner, *Your Church Can Grow* (Glendale: Regal, 1976.)

let each adopt a form of self-government.

Many Episcopal churches have three congregations—named by the hour of their worship on Sunday. Each is a distinct fellowship group and, when allowed to have some measure of control over the issues that count for it, contributes effectively to a healthy church. Wagner's advice is sound and serves to further explain the decline in numbers that follows the combining of Sunday worship services.

Even the common practice of having fewer worship services in the summertime may be unwise and psychologically frustrating for people who suddenly find themselves part of a different fellowship group. The fact that fewer services can accommodate the participants in the "off months" is undeniable, but the possibility that mixing primary fellowship groups may contribute to the decreased attendance and discomfort for those who do come is rarely considered.

Wagner's second and smaller building block is the cell, a group that offers the face-to-face intimacy of the primary family group. In the small church cell and congregation are one; in larger churches there may be two or three or four congregations, each of which will or should have numerous cells as the setting for primary relationships.

What makes all of this so vital is the strength of the basic, human, religious urges to be at one with others in a situation of dependable attachment to symbols and groups worthy of devotion. Men and women are social beings moved by psychological and spiritual needs for belonging. Lively and flourishing congregations are providing a sound fit between the needs and aspirations of the members and the climate of norms, goals, and resources in the congregation.

But people are different, and congregations are different. What does a good fit look like? How can some assessments be made of the hopes of the membership and the response of the church? In particular, what individual attributes and what organizational characteristics are most critical for the creation of a sound relationship between church and member? How is the nature of that relationship influenced by the sense of being in community or fellowship?

At this point it is important to remind ourselves that when we speak of a group, small or large, as a community, we are speaking of a special quality or form of group life. Graham Pulkingham, a man who has given leadership to the movement to renew the church through community, states that "as far as I'm concerned, the word 'community' needs to be replaced by the deepest meaning of what family is."[17] Pulkingham is emphasizing the quality of life that is highlighted by Dudley's comments about the small church as the single-cell group offering security and intimacy. We all belong to many groups, but only a few achieve for us this sense of closeness.

Social scientists have created a useful means of helping us to look at a congregation and make such distinctions. A. K. Rice and E. J. Miller of the Tavistock Institute in England have analyzed organizations using the distinction between (1) task groups—groups organized to do work or a particular job; and (2) sentient groups—groups that demand and receive loyalty from their members; that is, groups in which individuals invest sentiment and from which they derive personal support.[18]

Work-group boundaries and sentient-group boundaries may or may not coincide. A church finance committee whose task is to manage budget and finances may not be a sentient group for its members. An altar guild whose task it is to care for linens, vestments, and altar flowers is, in many congregations, a strong sentient group for most of its members. A sentient group is one to which we have an emotional attachment and identification. Other writers use the terms *reference group* or *primary group* to describe what Miller and Rice call sentient groups and what we will call a *church family group*.

The reference-group concept adds to our understanding by emphasizing two functions of a church family group.[19] The first is the notion that such groups help to shape our self-concept by

[17]"Interview with Graham Pulkingham on Creating Christian Family," *Sojourners Magazine,* May–June 1976, vol. 5, no. 5.
[18]A. K. Rice, and E. J. Miller, "Systems of Organization: Task and Sentient Systems and their Boundary Control" (London: Tavistock, 1967).
[19] K. Gershenfeld, *Groups: Theory and Experience* (Boston: Houghton Mifflin, 1973).

serving as a standard of comparison for our judgments and evaluations of ourselves and our world. Thus clergy colleague groups become a kind of looking glass, which individual pastors use to test and compare their view of social and self-reality. Second, membership in the group entails a set of social pressures that condition or shape individual behavior. Clergy often cite their membership in a colleague group as a way of reinforcing their commitment to a disciplined habit of study or prayer. It is the function of social pressure and its role as a standard of comparison that help to give the church family group what Dudley calls a culture-carrying capacity, for it is through processes such as these that an individual adopts the invisible, customary, and accepted beliefs and standards of the group.

A church is made up of groups. There are formal groups, such as the church board and official commissions. There are also informal groups, which form around shared interests, proximity, background, and common tasks. The informal groups may never be visibly defined or noticed, but they are very much still present and functioning. Both formal and informal groups can be distinguished by the degree to which they are task groups or family groups. A church located in a rapidly changing, heterogeneous community will find itself needing to structure a variety of task and family groupings. The greater the range and number of those groups, the more the church will have to structure processes for keeping the individual groups tied into the congregation as a whole.

A major test of the structure of any church is the degree to which each individual is enabled to freely join and participate in an association of other Christians. What happens to the new member who has not yet joined or who has not yet found a family home in the congregation is a crucial test of church structure. The extent to which the membership can be placed in a church family group and the extent to which all groups coexist in some harmony is an indication of the extent to which fellowship is present in the congregation.

The integrating structures of church life, or getting together and staying together

Whether engaged in the task of maintaining the buildings or in the tasks of welcoming new members, sharing a moment of crisis, or celebrating corporate worship, at all times and in all places the assembling of Christians is a free, voluntary, association. The extent to which an individual will feel attracted to and integrated into such a fellowship is the degree to which there is a match between the individual's hopes and values and the values and goals of the group.

Dean Hoge, a sociologist at Catholic University, has recently delineated from a review of research, as well as his own work, a generalized picture of middle-class church members and their basic value system.[20] His research confirms the concept of the fit between the person and the institution as central to commitment. This is crucial. A great many church leaders and groups continue to behave as if membership commitment is a value in and of itself—"If those people really loved the church, they would give more"—rather than the outward sign of the fact that people see participation as instrumental to the pursuit of their own hopes and values—"Perhaps the reason those folks aren't involved is that they can't see much congruence between what we stand for and what they are hoping to find."

Hoge's studies also underline the fact that the central goals and values of middle-class American adults are related to family, career, and standard of living. When there are health worries in the family, health quickly takes on equal importance. The picture that emerges from Hoge's research in the United Presbyterian Church is of a membership divided into two theological parties but united by values of family, career, and standard of living (see Table D).

Hoge also found that whether or not people felt their way of life in jeopardy (a sense of social threat) constituted an im-

---

[20]Dean R. Hoge, *Division in the Protestant House, The Basic Reasons Behind Intra-Church Conflict* (Philadelphia: Westminster, 1976).

portant factor in predicting their support or nonsupport of various church actions. "Persons who feel that their station and style of life are either actually or potentially threatened by hostile social forces want the church to provide a safe haven and to stay away from the types of social action that they assume would bring further change. Persons who feel more secure are more likely to advocate church social action. This is an important division in the church today."

Racial identity also made a difference in where people stood on specific church programs. Thus blacks whose theology on all other counts identified them with the Private Protestant camp gave actions such as fighting injustice high priority. When Hoge tested reactions to specific church actions inimical to middle-class values, race, attitudes about race, and the sense of psychological threat weighed as heavily as theological position in determining support or nonsupport.

Hoge's study gives us another lens to view the congregational problem of differentiation and integration. It vividly demonstrates why both the Presbyterian and United Methodist membership studies found that growing churches had structured an emphasis on Christian education and youth. Hart-

---

TABLE D
Public Protestants and Private Protestants

The two parties are united by values of family, career, standard of living. They agree on central goals of the importance of members' worship and nurture.

but

The two parties hold differing theological positions:

Public Protestants	Private Protestants
Hold a theology that:	Hold a theology that:
—sees the unity of the spiritual and material and makes no distinction between body and soul.	—regards human nature as a dualism of body and soul.
—takes seriously the social impact of institutions and culture on human freedom.	—stresses the free will of the individual as the main determinent of behavior.
—focuses on fulfillment in this life.	—focuses on fulfillment in the afterlife.
—favors social action as mission outreach.	—favors evangelism as social outreach.

man's research in the United Methodist Church showed "that church schools and churches which are growing have visibly and actively demonstrated concern for children and youth." Such activities demonstrate support and concern for family life and in so doing uphold the values Hoge has highlighted.[21]

From almost any point of view, people want a caring community that offers stability in family and personal nurture goals. The sense of community that is the foundation of such a congregation is continually threatened by the presence of individuals and groups with conflicting points of view. Lucky and rare is the congregation today that does not contain sizable numbers of each of Hoge's parties or all five of Hartman's audiences. If a local church organizes so that all individuals are always commingled in heterogeneous task groups dictated by some formal organization chart, the evidence is that church growth will suffer, conflict is likely, and the level of fellowship will remain low.

Conversations with the clergy of an aging suburban parish revealed that the leadership group split into two coequal centers of power. The old guard were long-term residents of the somewhat decayed suburban community. They had lived through two previous pastors, one of whom they saw as a hero, the other as a villain. The neighborhood continued to change, showing increasing racial and economic diversity. The pastor who had disappointed them had combined a vigorous social awareness with a leadership style that emphasized interpersonal awareness and an open, confrontational mode of communication. He preached and taught about the corporate and institutional injustice in our society. Those members he had attracted had drifted away from the church when his successor arrived. They were public Protestants, whose institutional church commitment, according to Hoge, is generally not very intense. Only the old guard stayed on, private Protestants intensely loyal to the parish and overjoyed by the successor pastor, who himself was a clear private Protestant, a vigorous, self-directed worker. His social concern efforts always carried strong evangelistic over-

---

[21]Hartman, *Membership Trends,* pp. 46–47.

tones, were centered on individual action, and did not threaten middle-class values. Much more than the first pastor, this man ran the show, remaining firmly the leader. The congregation could rely on him to be in charge and not to press them for personal self-disclosure or to propel them into settings of interpersonal conflict or uncertainty.

The third pastor of the two decades described this history with some bewilderment. His efforts had brought a new group on board—a group now coequal with the old guard and much more public Protestant, similar in values to the long-departed earlier group. Efforts to help the present groups work together were not going well. The old guard were complaining of the loss of community and fellowship. The new guard were impatient for more opportunities to make their presence known. Attempts to work through differences between the two groups aroused the old guard's fear of a return to the stresses of yesteryear when such conflict had seemed to them to be a priority goal of their public Protestant pastor. The present pastor knew that he was perceived as having public Protestant values and was also regarded as not strong enough as a leader.

This church boldly illuminates Hoge's categories and vividly illustrates the difficulty of creating and maintaining the ecology of church community. For the church to grow and to have a healthy sense of community there must be some congruence between the hopes and values of potential members and the norms and goals of the congregation. The greater the diversity in the community, the more the church must diversify to achieve a good fit. But as this illustration shows, the more the church differentiates itself, the more difficult is the task of adequate integration between church groupings. As the church adjusts itself to a changing culture and community so that people of differing backgrounds might find a home, it must also adjust itself to handle the increased needs for information, communication, and ritual occasions of oneness that have to be present for a wider sense of fellowship to exist.

The Invisible Stability of Norms and Roles

Two new concepts are critical to understanding a congregation's capacity to create a climate of attraction and integration. The concepts of norms and of roles are the keys to understanding the integrating, stabilizing forces of church life.

Norms are the informal, unwritten rules about what is and is not acceptable, "good" member behavior. Sometimes the word *norm* is used to refer to the idea or concept that is in people's minds concerning what members should or ought to do or be under certain circumstances. Defined in this manner, norms can refer both to behavior—what good members actually do—and to attitudes—what people think good members should think or do. Other writers use the concept of norms to refer only to actual behavior. The norm of the group is defined by the actual behaviors of the influential majority. The difference between a norm and a simple pattern of behavior rests in what happens when someone deviates and behaves differently. If it is simply the pattern of behavior of a church committee that the male group members wear coats and ties to the meetings, then the nonconformist in shirt sleeves will go relatively unnoticed. On the other hand, if the dress code is a group norm, then the individual is likely to be greeted with a number of slightly humorous but nevertheless pointed references to his attire.

Almost all churches have some formal policy concerning the requirements for a member in good standing. Norms are the informal requirements that an individual must adhere to in order to be acceptable. As a newly divorced woman in a family-oriented congregation said, "I know about norms—every time I try in a church setting to talk about my divorce, people get very uncomfortable and change the subject. I'm beginning to feel as if I don't really belong here anymore."

Norms usually develop slowly and imperceptibly. They are thus generally least apparent to the old timers and most visible to newcomers who have not yet been acculturated. The key elected leadership of one congregation were engaged in a discussion of the complaint of some of the newer members in the church that there was an "in-group–out-group" problem in the church. The leadership couldn't understand the meaning of these complaints. Statements were made and affirmed to the effect that all people could be a part of this church if they really wanted to make the commitment. As the leaders saw it, the door to the leadership in-group was always open, and anyone could walk through the door. Later in the same meeting a different concern arose, labeled core group burn-out. The group expressed its worry over the generally shared feeling of being overloaded and overpressured by the demands the church placed upon it.

This group and its two discussions illustrate a set of congregational norms in action. "Good" members of the church are members who not only give heavily of their time and money, they make this church central to their lives. Behaving in this fashion had become the price of election to the church board. In a sense, the role of leader had become defined by the role of the superlatively good member. These realities were invisible to the present leadership, who had paid the price willingly and gladly. They couldn't see any connection between their own problem of feeling burned out and the out-group concerns and complaints. It didn't occur to them that the strength and intensity of "good member commitment" norms had created an exclusivity to the leadership—an exclusivity informally but powerfully based upon a particular definition of what a church leader ought to be. The rewards of election and recognition went to those who fulfilled the norms. The sanction of remaining the outsider went to those who chose a different relation to the church.

In sum, some of the major characteristics of norms are:[22]

1. Norms usually develop around practices that are important to the group members. This doesn't mean that norms will always be objectively important to the church or that the practices in question will contribute to effectiveness. All that is necessary is that the behaviors seem important to the members.

---

[22]For a discussion of norms see Fritz Steele and Stephen Jenks, *The Feel of the Work Place* (Reading, Mass.: Addison-Wesley, 1977).

2. Not all group patterns of behavior constitute a norm. A norm is created by a set of rewards and punishments. Research shows that when a person expresses an opinion that deviates from the rest of the group, the individual receives increased communication from the group members as they try to bring the deviant into line.

3. Norms differ in intensity. Some will relate very strongly to areas that are strictly taboo.

4. Norms differ in the degree to which they apply to different individuals and groups. Some norms will apply only to one sex or only to newcomers; others (for instance, what we do in church when we pray) will apply to everyone.

5. Some norms pertain only to one person, such as the group leader or the minister. In this case the norms create a "role."

6. Norms can also be very specific or quite general in the behaviors they prescribe. It may be acceptable to arrive any time in the first fifteen minutes of the worship service and sit where you please, or it may be that the late arrival is expected to wait and be seated at a specific moment in a particular location.

The concept of roles is an equally important and related key to the informal structures of church life. The idea of role is a special application of the norm concept, for role refers to the shared expectations of group members regarding who is to do what and in what situations. Thus role refers to a set of norms that apply very specifically to the role occupant, such as the minister or the Sunday school teacher. A job description is a formal, written statement of the duties expected of the occupant of a particular job. The concept of role should bring to mind all the people who have expectations of a particular role as well as the person in the focal role and his or her experience of these informal, verbal and nonverbal, role pressures and expectations.

Norms and roles are particularly crucial in shaping the climate or culture of a congregation. Planned programs of education, worship, and fellowship are usually not the most potent bearers of Christian values present in the church. The total ecology of church life is the dominant teaching–healing instrument. It is the culture of the church—the amalgam of worship, fellowship, organizational practices, group experiences and architectural settings—that forms the central shaping influence upon the lives of the members. It is this total environment of rewards, attitudes, beliefs, practices, and values that is the primary source of nurture and challenge. The programs of church life, its worship and education, are simply aspects of the total life of the church, which in all its ways and means is creating a spiritual, intellectual, and affective field that continually engages the membership in life change.

John Westerhoff of Duke University has popularized this concept in the field of religious education and called it "religious socialization."[23] We believe that the key to assessing the learning that stems from the experience of socialization into congregational life is the church's existing system of norms and roles. Norms and roles are the most pervasive and powerful regulators of the behavior of group members. It is through them that the specialness or character of a church makes its impact upon the behavior of the members. The extent to which a church consciously and deliberately examines, creates, and enforces norms and roles congruent with its theology and mission is the most important of Christian education activities. Since norms and roles generally evolve in unconscious and invisible ways, this aspect of church structure is also most commonly ignored. The interrelationship of the various aspects of church structure is diagramed in Figure 2.

The experience of our membership in the church is the experience that teaches us what Christians say and do. Norms and roles are the cohesive forces that help keep us together as a community and give us distinctive character and personality. The new member, deciding whether and where to fit in, will most clearly experience the particular character of a local church and, hence, is the individual most likely to be aware of the role and norm structure.

---

[23]John H. Westerhoff and Gwen K. Neville, *From Generation to Generation* (Philadelphia: Pilgrim Press, 1974).

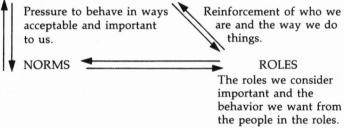

Figure 2. *Interrelationship of Church Structures.*

Summary

The structural component of the ministry system does not include just our formal-organizational charts and the buildings we inhabit. Structure and organization also include the patterns of our life together—the functioning of the constant assembling process of the people of God.

The structure of a church must be able to sense the different audiences present in the community, present a clear face to the community, and provide defined access to the church. The groups within a church can be differentiated into task groups and family groups; some groups will fulfill aspects of both functions. The norms and roles of these groups must be so differentiated as to provide a good initial fit with the constituencies present in the community. At the same time the integrating force of the church's identity must be expressed in norms and roles congruent with the stated theology and values of the church.

Above all, the church is a free, voluntary association in its essential structural nature. The elements of bureaucracy should not confuse or mislead us in the continuing quest for missionary structures fruitful to the great Commandment.

5

Leadership in the Local Church

Definitions and Assumptions

Leadership is a word with a wide assortment of meanings. Sometimes we use leadership to refer to those who occupy the role of leader. At other times when people speak of leadership, their discussion centers around the special traits of those who are proven leaders, of their capacity to generate loyalty and inspire confidence. Leadership can describe a set of functional tasks that must be performed if a group is to do its task and maintain itself as an organism. Broadly speaking, leadership can be regarded as the capacity to bring people together in the accomplishment of common goals. To some degree our discussion of leadership as one of the four major components of the ministry system will touch on all of these ways of understanding the terms; congregational leadership encompasses in quite everyday phenomena these diverse understandings.

An underlying assumption of our model is that church leadership is required to fulfill three basic tasks. The balance among these tasks will vary from congregation to congregation, depending upon its particular identity, structure, and community relationship. These three leadership tasks are:

1. To provide efficient organizational management. The brick-and-mortar, bureaucratic aspects of church life demand careful, efficient administration and execution.

2. To provide effective guidance for the gathering church, helping the membership clarify directions and associate

together with a free commitment to the mission of the church.

3. To provide authentic spiritual direction—congruent, authoritative teaching, preaching, counsel, and witness in order to help people know themselves and the world through the eyes of faith.

Where any one of these leadership functions is missing or weak, a church's ministry will suffer. When any two of these functions are weak or out of balance, the resulting problems are usually grievous for the life of the congregation. Where any or all of the three functions fall primarily upon clergy or laity rather than being responsibly shared, the church will experience weakness in the execution of its leadership functions. The tasks are further delineated in the model of parish leadership functions in Figure 3.

A second fundamental assumption is that all three leadership functions involve, at their core, the question of leader–member relationships. There is no leadership without followership. The quality of the relationship between leaders and members is the single most important determinant of leadership effectiveness. It will be a constant focus in the discussion which follows.

Effective Association Leadership

We stressed earlier that the institutional church comprises both an association and its attendant bureaucracy. This distinction has several implications for the function of leadership in ministry.

Leadership in a voluntary association is with the consent of the governed. The leader works for the people and not vice versa. Association leadership is far more political in nature than it is managerial. This difference is graphically represented by examining contrasting participatory planning processes.

Churches often install broad-based planning procedures as if they were bureaucratic organizations. The participatory nature of such processes can be very elaborate. Mounds of data are accumulated, questionnaires and meetings are bred at high

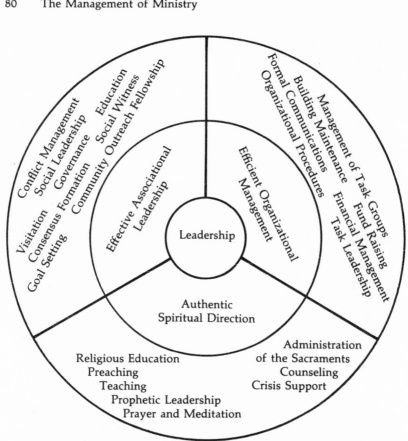

Figure 3. Model of Parish Leadership Functions.

rates; the data are sifted, discussed, sifted again; goals and objectives are formed. Such processes often lead to short-run bursts of volunteer energy. Goals are generated. There is certainly a shared experience of participation and involvement, which lingers as a permanent positive legacy. It is our recurrent experience, however, that this managed style of planning usually ends in a cloud of procedural boredom. The weight of accumulated print soon becomes a symbolic reminder of the despair of the dispirited majority of the congregation.

In startling contrast is the effectiveness of this same planning process if it is infused with visionary leadership. "Associations are power groups. Their members differentiate into power sub-groups for purposes of argument and debate. It is the art of leadership to facilitate this debate."[1] We are describing the kind of leadership that is sensitive to the feelings and views of the constituents and doesn't always have to refer back to them or take an opinion poll to act, and can inspire people to higher goals and values than stem from self-interest or attitude surveys. It is the type of leadership that forges a consensus rather than simply searching for an amenable, smoothed-over, majority point of view.

A congregation needs leadership, stemming from both clergy and laity, which can arouse the constituent elements of the church in a spirit-filled call to God's mission. Inevitably there will be conflict, because groups differ in their aspirations. These differences will be expressed in power relationships between groups and individuals, and the leadership must be prepared to mediate.

The governance processes of the church, with their charters and constitutional elective procedures, are ways associations evolve to provide frameworks and limits for the expression of power. Church conventions and the annual meetings of congregations are moments when the associative nature of the church is most visible. Within constitutional limits power groups vie to elect the leadership they want and seek. This political arena is vital for our health. Bureaucratic and managerial attitudes and practices are to be avoided in this area of the church's life. There has been a recent tendency in the Episcopal Church to remove the political element from the election of bishops and to replace it with rational management selection processes. A proposal we would favor is to more openly acknowledge that elections are times to allow those who would take this position of leadership to exercise their leadership in the attempt to be elected.

The tendency to gravitate toward rational, bureaucratic management process is prevalent in our society. In the church,

---

[1]Elliott Jaques, *A General Theory of Bureaucracy* (London: Heinemann, 1976).

as the Body of Christ, all are equals. It is this associative quality that provides the freedom to explore belief, to achieve intimacy, and to express love. Clergy are not merely professional employees. They are equal members of the Body.

Efficient Bureaucratic Management

The church does contain definite bureaucratic elements. Superior–subordinate relationships of accountability in task-differentiated organizations are certainly appropriate characteristics of most national church agencies.

Such elements exist even at the local church level. It is often hard to distinguish where organizational management ends and association leadership begins. Many times, of course, actual leadership behavior will be accomplishing both functional ends. A church committee planning for the fall education program is a situation where it is difficult to make a clear distinction. Nevertheless, it soon becomes apparent that there is a consistent strand of task leadership and management that must be performed for the group to do its job. Goals must be outlined, schedules prepared, staff recruited and trained, publicity prepared and released, follow-up supervision must occur—the list of organizational management tasks to be accomplished is lengthy and important. The most exciting educational plan can founder if these details are not efficiently managed. Eventually even the most energetic congregation becomes dispirited if people keep stumbling over the obstacles of inefficient organizational management.

Some clergy frequently lament the difficulty they have in holding people accountable for work to be done: "If people say they will do a job, why do they not follow through and get it done?" On one level this complaint can be read as a minister's wish that people were employees and not volunteers—a wish that the intrinsic forces of volunteer motivation could be replaced by the coercive powers of the employer–employee relationship.

On another level, however, it is our sense that many clergy simply do not understand the full scope of the management task. Many seminaries still teach a course entitled Parish Administration—a course on handling the organizational details and arrangements of church life. This is a misleading and narrow view to be perpetuating. Just organizing a task group and sending it into the usual troubled seas of church life is not a functional view of the management task. The traditional definitional categories of management are:[2]

1. Planning (Setting goals)

2. Organizing (Recruiting)

3. Staffing (Training)

4. Directing (Supervision)

5. Controlling (Evaluation)

Planning means creating a plan. A plan has objectives, strategies, budget policies, and procedures. Planning involves the conceptualization of future courses of action. Program planning is a necessity in church life. Strategic, long-range planning for the overall direction of a church may or may not be necessary; it can never be a substitute for associative leadership.

Organizing is sometimes thought of as planning the plan. This is the area of administration that involves making the arrangements necessary to carry out the plan. It means deciding whether we need two task groups of six people each or one large committee, and who will be the chairperson.

Accomplishing these two steps of planning and organizing is as far as many clergy go in their administrative view of the organizational side of church life. As a consequence the task groups so organized rapidly get into severe difficulties. *Staffing* is necessary for work groups. Individuals need orientation and training. Roles are not automatically clear and unambiguous. Effective work procedures usually appear only after training and practice.

Once the group is working, problems will inevitably occur.

[2]R. Alec MacKenzie, "The Management Process in 3–D," *Harvard Business Review,* November–December 1969.

Conflicts will surface; communication gaps will appear. *Directing* means exercising managerial leadership so that problems are solved and the flow of communication is reestablished.

Evaluation is a more neutral word for many people than the management word *controlling*. Whatever we call the function, the need to learn from what we have done in order to guide future action is essential.

The maintenance of the fabric of church life depends upon the utilization of limited volunteer energy and funds in efficient work. In most churches 90 percent of this work is done by task groups and committees. Efficient and effective management of their work requires clear goals, wise recruitment, sound training, continuous problem solving, and timely evaluation. There is no substitute for this hard work. Church leaders continue to search for stewardship campaigns that will run by themselves, hoping that a level of commitment can be attained so that the leadership tasks of work management can be ignored. This hope is seldom realized. As one pastor expresses it, "The reason we hire professional fund raisers isn't that they have some magical solution to how to raise money. It is that they make us do the things we know need doing but often just don't do." The same can be said for every area of the church's life that requires organized and coordinated effort for the maintenance of the institution.

Authentic Spiritual Direction

Paul Tillich has said that church leaders "gain absolute authority because of the absolute character of what they stand for."[3] We wish to describe three ways in which the "absolute" nature of leadership becomes manifest in the conduct of church life. Together these three areas shape the core church leadership function of authentic spiritual direction. The three areas are: (1) The leader as bearer of the holy; (2) leadership and theology; and (3) Leadership in the shaping of communitas.

---

[3]Paul Tillich, "The Nature of a Liberating Conscience," *Conscience— Theological and Psychological Perspectives,* ed. C. Ellis Nelson (New York: Newman Press, 1973).

The leader as bearer of the holy

John Fletcher, former president of Inter/Met, a creative Washington, D. C., experiment in theological education, has advanced an enormously important insight regarding the relationship between congregation and pastor. Fletcher and his colleagues investigated the central problems between clergy and laity. In twenty-some congregations the most critical issue they uncovered Fletcher has come to call religious authenticity.[4] Fletcher is calling to our attention that a minister, rather than being religiously authenticated once, at the time of ordination, must be authenticated in each new congregational setting. Three stages, with their accompanying crises, constitute the work of authentication:

1. Testing Personal Strength. A period of mutual self-discovery, marked by mutual testing, mutual probing of the relationship, and denial of the stress involved. The disappointment and pain can lead to a pattern of permanent avoidance. This crisis of human authenticity, if resolved on the basis of mutual care and realistic candor, leads to the next stage.

2. Professional Authenticity. "The second crisis point of authentication of clergypersons begins around the issue of whether anyone is going to invite them into a serious religious relationship." Once people begin sharing their pastoral and religious concerns, the pastor may be overwhelmed by the flood of human need. Overdependence on the pastor may be one result. Another outcome can be the submergence of the pastor, overwhelmed by his own need to be everything to everybody. "Not until the clergyperson's own experience in the congregation has the quality of living dependently on God, rather than the congregation living dependently on the leader, is the crisis transcended."

---

[4]John Fletcher, *Religious Authenticity in the Clergy, Implications for Theological Education* (Washington, D.C.: Alban Institute, 1977).

3.   Particular Authenticity. This is a period of harmonious growth for pastor and people. It is a time of self-definition for the minister, who is now free to clarify basic strengths and abilities. Rather than seeing these activities as a cop-out, the congregation willingly collaborates in the definition.

One implication of Fletcher's three stages is that the absolute, setapart character of the minister, although symbolized by ordination, is, in fact, an achievement of a set of interactions between leaders and members. A leader becomes a bearer of the holy as the result of having worked through a set of dilemmas and issues with members of the congregation. A second implication is that these stages of authentication represent milestones along the path of faith development as traveled by all members of a congregation. While, as one seminarian expressed it, there is a seeming fascination with the person and place of the minister in church life, we see the issues that explain this fascination as critical for all members and all leaders.

A fundamental issue raised by the progression and content of the three stages is the correlation between people's dependence on the leader and their dependence on God. The wish to live dependently on the leader is of a piece with the wish to live dependently on God. Blind submission to the leader leads easily to blind faith. Leaders help to develop members with a freely chosen, thoughtful faith by understanding and not succumbing to the individual and group pressures created by the unconscious wish to be cared for by an external authority. These pressures particularly focus upon the ordained minister as leader because that role is central in church life. The same forces, however, are operative when any individual, lay or ordained, moves clearly into the limelight of church life.

Seemingly untouched by any studies of parish ministry, entirely ignored by theological studies of the church and its mission, and largely ignored by social psychology is this most critical and abiding force shaping the relation between pastor and people. Freud uncovered this force, which operates on the unconscious, primary level.[5] The group on this level sees the leader as omnipotent and omniscient. They are responding, unconsciously, to a longing for "the magical protection, the participation in omnipotence, the 'oceanic feeling' that they enjoyed when they were loved and protected by their parents."[6]

When a new minister moves into groups in the church, what is manifest is the interpersonal behavior and spoken themes of the groups' activities. What is not manifest is the intrapersonal underworld brought by each individual. Whatever might be the pastor's rational theology or leadership style, whether the content of the discussion is altar flowers, money, burial practices, or the past rector, the group setting is swamped by latent forces never discussed and invisible to the members. The forces of organizational life, the patterns of group and leader development, an individual's spiritual development—all of these life processes are integrally affected by subconscious self-expression. In everyday language these are the forces of irrationality, or the expressions of the unconscious. A denominational official, in commenting on a proposed schema for the structure of the local congregation, said that it seemed to presuppose complete rationality. This assumption of rationality is commonplace. But it is impossible for us to understand what is happening to a new church leader without taking seriously the forces of anxiety and irrational fear. Nor can we understand the relationship of ordained and lay leadership to the ministry of the parish in the formation of values and the shaping of life styles without examining such psychic processes as projection and transference.

Our thesis is that the relationship between pastor and people is a paradigm of the relationship between people and God. Plumbing the depths of the pastor–people relationship is a means of illuminating the nature of the religious quest. If we think of a person as a whole system, then it is apparent that the depths contain theological, psychological, and sociological

<hr>

[5]Sigmund Freud, *Group Psychology and the Analysis of the Ego.* Standard Edition, vol. 18 (London: Hogarth Press, 1960).
[6]Ernest Becker, *The Denial of Death* (New York: Free Press, 1973).

realities that are separable only as intellectual constructs and not as phenomena of direct experience. We are confident that God is present in life and that the understanding of human experience, from whatever source, does not have to be reductionist but can expose the infinite vistas of life. As Scripture shows us time and again, each human relationship can be a window into the mysteries of the relationship between God and humanity. Ministers are people of authority within the sacred setting of a congregation because they partake of the basic processes of projection that are so much a part of the religious quest.

Freud consistently expressed the view that the deepest traceable sources of religious need lead back to infantile wishes for an all-powerful father. "The derivation of religious needs from the infant's helplessness and the longing for the father aroused by it seems to me to be incontrovertible, especially since the feeling is not simply prolonged from childhood days, but is permanently sustained by fear of the superior power of Fate."[7] If ministers or lay leaders experience the congregation as wishing them to be omniscient, nourishing, loving, protective, controlling, freeing, and omnipotent, it is because of their needs to attribute those powers to God and hence to God's representative. Freud's insights, in spite of the claims sometimes made about them, do not explain away religious belief and practice. His thought does point to the depths of human experience within which lies encounter with the Divine.

In "The Nature of a Liberating Conscience," a little noticed essay, Paul Tillich clearly spelled out the theological implications of the psychological process of projection. Tillich asserted that we all experience an unconditional demand, an all-embracing, life-enveloping, moral imperative. There is an essential moral character to the universe, made known to us in the silent call of conscience and in the transmitted wisdom of the centuries through law, custom, and social mores. Beneath imposed systems of ethics, behind the clarity and confusion of individ-

---

[7] *Civilization and its Discontents,* (1930) vol. XXI, in *The Complete Psychological Works of Sigmund Freud,* tr. and ed. James Strachey (London: Hogarth Press, 1953).

ual conscience, Tillich argues, is an essentially human belief that life does have a normative character that transcends the expediency of each new era.

This essential and abiding belief Tillich calls the screen of unconditional demand. It is upon this screen that we project the disturbing, unresolved ambivalences of our childhood relationship to those who represented the authority of "ought" and "should" in our early years. Psychotherapy can help us to see more clearly the images we flash upon the screen, the flickering lights and shadows of our past. Psychotherapy does not dissolve the screen itself, rather, it should help us to recognize the demonic and neurotic identification of limited human perception with Divine revelation. Projection confuses religious belief with God, and the pastor is experienced as the source of religious authority. The needs for the control of fate, of anxiety, and of guilt lead us to a false identification of the existential means of control with the transcendent itself.

Thus new ministers experience an unconscious, irrational demand from people in the congregation that they be the secure, saving defense against the anxiety and fear of life. If the demand is met, the minister becomes idolized, revered as an essential bulwark of religious faith. If the minister fails in responding to the demand, then the congregation may feel frustrated and hostile. As Tillich pointed out, the journey of faith lies through and not around these forces. God offers not a refuge from life but the courage to live fully into self and life.

The fascination with the pastor, the dynamic power present in the stages through which pastor and people move in the authentication of the pastor's ministry, help us to see the awesome power of the parish setting. The local congregation awakens the primal forces buried deep within us. The setting gives us the opportunity to recapitulate with truth and love the conflicts, ambivalences, and frustrated wishes of family life. The setting gives us a new chance to *know* that God does not call us to neurotic and demonic solutions.

Jesus said that we must be born again. The congregation is the family, and its leaders the parents during the new birth process. If the Christian cannot move beyond to see the psychological and religious distortion in remaining dependent on the concrete presence of church, pastor, and people, then the birth process is aborted. The thread of existence is resolved, once more, by giving over to others the courage to be. Psychoanalysts call this phenomenon transference. It involves submitting oneself to an external object, trying to control life by transfer of one's own human qualities to an externality. To lose the transference object is to lose oneself. The pastor, the congregation, the communion, the creedal tenets—any and all can be such objects. We have focused on the new pastor relationship because it so clearly highlights the pervasive presence of the transference phenomenon in church life. Why the fascination with the minister? Because, in Ernest Becker's words, "the transference object always looms larger than life size because it represents all of life and hence all of one's fate. The transference object becomes the focus of the problem of one's freedom because one is compulsively dependent on it; it sums up all other natural dependencies and emotions."

Whether met with the soothing waters of adulation or the rude shock of cold hostility, the pastor faces a clear dilemma. The minister's credit as a leader is dependent on establishing a relationship with the congregation predicated on loyalty and trust. People must give authority to the minister before the ministry is possible. The temptation is to use this to achieve a productive, efficient, brick-and-mortar congregation. The dependency can be falsely used to create volunteer energy and commitment.

I remember an early church experience, in which one of the first people to appear at the church office was a quiet and energetic middle-aged woman, whom I will call Edith. During the previous pastor's tenure, Edith had taken special training in a pilot educational project. She was immediately recognizable as a pillar of the church. Her devotion to the church and her friendship with my predecessor was apparent. My first fear was that she would not like me, that her loyalty to the still-present ghost of the previous pastor would never be transfered to me. I was greatly relieved when she began spending time around the church and continued her heavy volunteer commitment. When she also chose to share some of her life and to ask for my advice and wisdom, I was even more affirmed.

Months went by, and only gradually did some other issues come to mind in my relationship with this woman. Edith was married, a nurse, and had some strong beliefs about the quality of life in her community. Somehow, these other commitments were always slighted, although she was seldom without the time and energy for her pastor and church. The net result of her life in the church was a continued deficit in her work, family, and community life. I began to wonder about the life force she seemed to have transfered onto me and the congregation. Her relationship to me and to the church seemed beneficial in the way an aspirin or a cane is helpful: She was aided, relieved, but not transformed. Something made me trust the relationship enough to raise the issue with Edith. I said that in some ways I felt used; that though I appreciated her loyalty and devotion to the church, and though I, too, needed her friendship, still the outcome seemed that her life was increasingly pale beyond the circle of her congregational involvement. In that moment a new relationship was born. Edith's initial reaction was anxiety and anger. But a struggle began—with herself, with me, with her husband, with her job, with God. Over the months and years a different Edith emerged, capable of saying no to me and to the church, able to move to new levels of intimacy with her husband; an Edith whose natural talents and abilities now found expression beyond the bounds of the congregation.

Rather than being an isolated incident, this vignette of a specific transference situation points, in Ernest Becker's words, to a "universal passion." Both the fearful retreat from the deep shadows of life and the often heroic attempts to make life right, to transcend one's self, make some sort of projective transference as necessary a part of the human condition as curiosity, hunger, or doubt. Though more immediately apparent in Edith's situation, the issue is always present as the central dynamic in the stages of movement between pastor and people. The pastor is coping, for good or ill, with the intricate web of unconscious, hidden, transference patterns. From this perspective Fletcher's three stages of clergy authentication can be amplified and seen not only as stages through which a new pastor must move in relation to the congregation but also, and more importantly, as stages in the journey of faith development.

The individual Christian's relationship to the church involves change and development over time. Initially the person commits to the church as it represents a setting that provides both security and meaning. The stronger this initial commitment, the more the pastor and the church seem necessary and omnipotent. Church members are severely tempted in this phase of the relationship to go along with the assumptions of their projection: "I didn't even have to tell the pastor I was ill; he just seemed to know." If things continue this way, the path to God is blocked by the mutual subversion of pastor and people maintaining the illusion that this group and this leader represent a perfectly dependable solution to life's anxieties. On the other hand, if church leaders are not dependable and authoritative (as opposed to authoritarian), if initiative and firm leadership are nowhere in their guidance of the congregation, then people may never take the first step of commitment from which all else must follow.

The second stage of the Christian journey made manifest in the relationship between pastor and people is one of inquiry and explanation. The work of this period involves an exploration and sharing of the mutual concerns of our dependent relationships. Expressions of love, respect, disappointment, anger, fears of loss, and hopes for protection become issues to be examined and honored. In the first stage often simple explanations will suffice; complexity cannot be understood and represents the failure of leadership to be clear. Self-study and self-knowledge are seen as nonsense. There is a search for cure-alls and "patent medicine" remedies. In the second stage of Christian life together, these assumptions must be challenged with a dependable facing of the facts of Christian living—of the real obstacles to community that will always exist among us. In this stage there is less fear that our strong emotions will overwhelm us. Disappointments between pastor and people can be examined rather than having to be contained. Pastors should not be surprised that their first or second attempts to initiate their own evaluation or a mutual examination of expectations between clergy and laity end in failure. If the previous pastor has unwittingly gone along with the assumptions of omnipotence, the task of moving any substantial proportion of the congregation into this second stage can be formidable indeed. The Alban Institute explorations of pastorate startups have confirmed the depression experienced by new pastors who seem surrounded by groups with distorted and unrealistic perceptions of themselves and the church. The clergy tended to feel alone and abandoned.[8]

Movement into and through the second stage of exploration and authentication is necessary to release both pastor and people for their true ministries. The third stage means recognizing the congregation as people living and working in the world outside of the church and the pastor as a fallible minister to the people of God as they gather to awaken and deepen their dependence upon the Triune God, who always transcends the demands and dependencies of our present situation. For both leader and member, here is where religious authentication of ministry is finally ordained.

Leadership and Theology

During the recent election of a Bishop in the Episcopal Church, a theological interpretation of the election process was sent to the people of the Diocese. The paper was drafted by a priest who was a prominent elected official in the Diocese. Contained in what was otherwise a sensitive and informative document was this statement: "As with many of you I am an amateur theologian—a parish priest, not a professor."

This apologetic statement reflects a feeling almost universal among clergy. It stands as an arrow pointing to the heart of the theological dilemma in the ministry of the church. Imagine receiving a letter from your family doctor proclaiming that "like many of you I am only an amateur healer, not a professor." The absurdity would be apparent.

Dr. John MacQuarrie has defined theology "as the study which through participation in and reflection upon a religious faith, seeks to express the content of this faith in the

---

[8]Roy M. Oswald, "Pastorate Start-up," *Action Information,* March 1977 (Alban Institute). Vol. iii, no. 1.

clearest and most coherent language available."[9]

The functional meaning of this definition for parish life was illustrated in a meeting of lay congregational leaders. One man, a city planner, was describing the motivations that had led him to become active as a leader in his congregation. "I knew," he said, "that I was looking for something that was missing in my life, and I felt that by becoming more active, by getting close to the center of the life of the church, I would find what it was that was missing—a something I could not even define for myself. And so I became a trustee, and what I found was a job vastly more complex than I had assumed. The brick-and-mortar tasks of running a volunteer organization are far more complicated and time consuming than an uninvolved person could ever know—at the same time what I didn't find was whatever it is that is beyond bricks and mortar." The purpose of theology is to describe in clear language the content of that which is beyond the bricks and mortar of congregational life. The task of theology is inherent in the task of ministry. It is an essential leadership task in the management of ministry.

Recently a seminary field-work student phoned to ask for help. He said that his task was to work with the Christian education committee of his field-work congregation and that he was bewildered by the difficulty he was having. "I can't seem to explain the nature of Christian education in any satisfactory way to this group. I really don't know what my ministry is with them, and they've got me confused about Christian education in the parish." This prospective pastor was asking for a theological guide to help him speak and behave in ways that would clarify the educational task of the church. One part of his group was adamant that education had to do with the knowledge of Scripture. Another subgroup seemed equally adamant that an exploration of crucial life issues was the most relevant and faithful way of describing Christian education.

This Christian education committee at work illustrates a typical church setting, in which individuals are gathered to decide the specific ways and means of running a church school.

---

[9]John MacQuarrie, *Principles of Christian Theology* (New York: Scribner's, 1966).

The group is seeking to describe for themselves and to produce for their children that which is beyond the bricks and mortar. One theological word that points the way is *salvation*. By following this Christian education committee and the concept of salvation, we can discover the excitement and difficulty of theology.

It is easy to see that this group is, in part, engaged in a discourse related to their understanding of salvation. They are debating how their children may be brought up knowing the fruits of redemption. One person believes that the knowledge and expression of Scripture is essential; another argues that only by helping the child to deepen its sense of self in life crisis will the saving power of God become real. What is probably common to all in the group is that the discussion of what is best for their children is an external projection of their own experience and understanding of salvation. Each person is present not just to do volunteer church school work or to build what is right for the children in the congregation. Though such feelings are seldom brought to consciousness and even less often articulated, each individual is seeking to move through the bricks and mortar to an experience of God as saviour.

The Bible roots God's saving actions in concrete experience:

I sought the Lord, and he answered me, and delivered me from all my fears. Look to him and be radiant; so your faces shall never be ashamed. The poor man cried, and the Lord heard him, and saved him out of all his troubles. The Lord is near to the broken-hearted, and saves the crushed in spirit (Psalm 34:4–6, 18, RSV).

Salvation in the New Testament points much more deeply to a transcendent and spiritual dimension. Thus St. Paul writes to the congregation in Thessalonica:

But we are bound to give thanks to God always for you, brethren beloved by the Lord, because God chose you from the beginning to be saved through sanctification by the Spirit and belief in the truth. To this he called you through our gospel, so that you may obtain the glory of our Lord Jesus Christ (II Thess. 2:13–14, RSV).

As even the earthly language of the Old Testament makes apparent, the theologian is dealing with nonsensuous experience. Salvation has no shape. It cannot be packaged, touched, smelled, or seen. The fearful, ashamed, and broken-hearted self lies deep in the mystery of the human spirit.

Langdon Gilkey has stated that the purpose of theology is to help us understand the appearance of the holy in our experience. He adds, "If the holy seems not at all to appear, then it is natural that discourse about it should seem irrelevant, meaningless and empty."[10] Certainly the pastor had described the debate of this Christian education committee as often irrelevant and empty. Environmental debate seemed a foolish pastime until the invisible pollutants in the air began to burn our throat and eyes. Can we understand what has not yet appeared? How can words mediate an experience never realized?

Theology as dogma has no problem; the theologian tells the group the answer. Theology as dogma contains the correct answer as to the nature of salvation and the consequent definition of Christian education. Most theological writing has operated on this approach. The correlation between experience and heritage becomes a process of translation into the latest popular or intellectual idiom. Both ordained and lay leaders regard themselves as amateur theologians and eagerly look for the newest theological "container" in hopes it will make the bridge between personal experience and the content of the Christian tradition. When the function of theology was to clearly articulate a faith based in the actual religious experience of the community, the container model was appropriate. This situation is long dead.

Today a new model of theological leadership is needed. Theology needs to be visualized as a dynamic tool or probe, which would pass on a method for unfolding human experience to its depths. The expert theologian is the individual able to help people move beneath the veneer to the deep-grained passions of love, justice, and immanence of the Eternal.

Most theological language used among church people actu-

---

[10]Langdon Gilkey, *How the Church Can Minister to the World Without Losing Itself* (New York: Harper & Row, 1964).

ally functions as jargon, or "official" language. The words are employed to designate the boundaries of group membership. The use or nonuse of a particular vocabulary is an identification badge designating group membership.

For example, one recent meeting turned out to be evenly composed of charismatic-pentecostal Episcopalians and liberal-humanist Episcopalians. The theological language employed by each subgroup was radically different. Within ten minutes it was evident that the language had become a name tag, effectively labeling subgroup membership. Complaints could be heard around the edges of the meeting about the way others used or did not use theological language. No concern was expressed about the need to talk about the religious realities toward which the words are supposed to point. As in primitive tribes, the language had become a means of reinforcing the tribal boundary against the evil encroachment of outsiders.

Beyond this boundary-maintenance function, the church's present theological language is rarely used by Christian people except in official functions such as worship, sermons, and study groups. In discussions of the Christian education committee case with seminarians and parish clergy, the standard theological language of the church is rarely invoked. Rather, what the pastors notice are such issues as:

> The nature of the pastor's leadership, particularly the use of authority.
>
> The personal agenda of the members.
>
> The lack of expression of, and interest in, the needs of the children.
>
> The impersonal expression of the needs of the group members.
>
> Group members' seeming lack of trust in one another.

These issues are noticed because they are real and powerful, and must be accounted for in any theological method. Official theological language is dead if it is a set of labels unconnected to such experience. At the same time a theology that stopped at this level of group and interpersonal activity would be a travesty. The midwife of theology is the bearer of the Holy. The birthplace of true theology lies beyond rationality in the place where the bush burns but is not consumed.

What is needed is a rigorous method by which a group under stress can begin to unfold for its members the experience and meaning of God's immanent presence. The contribution of theology is not new vocabulary. Theology must become a guide rather than remaining an interpreter.

The most guarded side of many an American's life is his or her spiritual journey. Exposing one's sexual life has become lucrative for the rich and famous, and routine party conversation for the poor and ordinary, but even those Christian congregations that have become settings for human intimacy and interpersonal candor remain rigidly silent about the private religious journey. In the course of her master's thesis, a religious educator, Jean Haldane interviewed in depth twenty people in a local congregation, focusing on the individual's religious journey and how it is influenced by membership in the congregation.[11] Among the many important findings of this study was Haldane's discovery that, without exception, the individuals interviewed stated this was the first time they had ever been asked to talk about their own experience with God. In fact, they expressed doubt and wonder that the church would even be interested.

Urban T. Holmes has stated that there is a need "to insist that seminaries teach a method of rigorous intellectual reflection upon the felt experience of God, in order that this experience may possess a clarity and balance that may be shared with others."[12] The first step in the direction Holmes is pointing is that we begin to talk with one another about our own religious experience. If God is indeed at work in the world, it is time to live into that faith by exercising our atrophied powers of discernment. People's usual mode of dealing with questions of personal religion was characterized by one person Haldane in-

---

[11]Jean Haldane, *Religious Pilgrimage* (Washington, D. C.: The Alban Institute, 1975).
[12]Urban T. Holmes, "The Seminary as Method," *The St. Luke's Journal*, September 1973, vol. XVI, no. 4.

terviewed, who said, "When you say something [that you believe or that matters to you] either someone argues with you, or they so agree that there is nothing more to talk about!" Another mode many of us have experienced is a verbal deluge of witness to Jesus, which soon silences the personal exploration. The persistent forces of institutional life have gradually brought the church to the point where intellectual assent and organizational allegiance have displaced the opportunity for personal and communal reflection upon one's spiritual journey.

Elizabeth Kubler-Ross has brought about a revolution in our understanding of death by listening to the dying. People had been dying for a long time, but no one had listened and asked of their experience as Kubler-Ross has.

In the child's world of learning, there is not only the means of understanding how children learn but also the means of enhancing that learning. By acutely insightful observation of young children as they learn, psychologist Jean Piaget has developed a profound base for the teaching–learning process.

We sometimes find ourselves feeling and acting as if we must import God into people's lives. In fact, God is not dependent upon us or the church. If God seems not to be there, it is because we do not have the eyes to see and the ears to hear. We have come to see, in church after church, the degree to which we talk about God but never, ever explore the actuality of our personal faith, practice, and experiences. Each of us does have a religious journey. With whatever words are ours, no matter which directions that journey has taken, the shared reflection on these experiences constitutes an essential element in theology as practice.

Words, however, are only sounds we utter to symbolize reality as perceived by the speaker. A foreign language is a different set of symbols for the same realities. Church members are usually foreigners to one another when they try to talk theology for the words do not possess common symbolic meaning. Exploration and reflection upon our religious journey will help overcome the language barrier. The best way, though, to learn a foreign language is to immerse oneself in the language, usually by going to live in that country. We have stressed thus far that theologians have been stuck in the interpreter's role and must instead move to the role of guide into the land of theological language—the land of religious experience. This makes it apparent that just listening and talking are not enough. The felt experience of God, as perceived by each speaker, must rest behind the spoken word. Haldane found a widespread fear of being judged in the people she interviewed. People shared a general nervousness about the rightness and worthwhileness of their experience. It is possible this fear is only a hesitancy to speak in front of others of matters personal and seldom discussed. We believe the fear has deeper roots. We believe it more closely akin to the fear people have of passion and emotion. More specifically, we believe that this fear is the anxiety connected with the internal mental process of experiencing deep emotions, recognizing the emotion, and putting it into words. It is the anxiety connected with the emergence into consciousness of what our sub-conscious says may be unacceptable or overwhelming. We are talking about what happens in the process of knowing an experience which threatens to carry us beyond the carefully bounded limits of daily life.

A friend has a classic story about this subject. It happened nearly twenty years ago, one summer when he was working as a student chaplain in a mental hospital, in a clinical pastoral education program required of seminary students. He tells about a pleasant interview he had with a very charming woman patient:

In her late thirties, she was married and had three school age children. She was one of the friendliest, most congenial persons I have ever met. We talked for close to an hour that afternoon in what was for me a completely enjoyable visit. She told me about her husband and his job . . . how they happened to meet and get married. We talked about her children, their schools and the PTA. She told me about her church and wanted to know about mine. She was interested in me: my home, family, education, my work at the hospital, my opinions about many things, my plans for the future. About her illness, she explained that a couple of months earlier, a nervous breakdown had put her in the hospital, but that she expected to go home any day now. Assuring her that she seemed perfectly fine to me and would undoubtedly be allowed to go home soon, I left that afternoon, feeling really good to have found among the patients this delightful person who was doing so well.

58742

The next morning I saw her again in a staff meeting. The staff was gathered to decide whether or not she could go home. They wanted to discuss this matter with her. She was perfectly composed and polite. As she told how the hospital had helped her, the gratitude and warm feelings which she had for the staff seemed very genuine. The way she talked about her homesickness for her husband and children brought tears to some eyes in that room.

Sitting close by was a crusty old German psychiatrist, who seemed totally unimpressed. He made it obvious that her story bored him by yawning openly and audibly. His rudeness went beyond this to interrupting, blowing cigar smoke in her face, and once belching out loud. Unruffled by this vulgar behavior, the gracious lady remained polite and friendly. She answered all of the questions asked by the chief psychiatrist. As was the custom he opened the floor to any member of the staff who had a question or wanted to comment. The German doctor tore into the patient like Perry Mason interrogating a hostile witness. His questions were sarcastic. He sneered and groaned at her answers, cutting her short before she could finish. He not only challenged everything she said, he did it in a way that was coarse, crude and grossly unfair. He insinuated in a dozen different ways that she was not to be believed or trusted. Throughout this unbelievably brutal attack, the woman remained resolutely polite. Everyone in that room was furious except her. Finally, the old doctor slumped back in his chair out of breath from the effort. He looked away as though he had lost interest in the matter. He seemed unaware that 25 people were staring daggers at him. There followed a silence broken by the chief psychiatrist sending someone out for a mirror.

He asked the patient how she felt. She said, "Fine . . . never better, really." "Don't you feel angry?" he asked. "Not at all," she answered. "Aren't you even a little annoyed at someone in this room?" "No," she said, "I don't always understand what you are doing, but I couldn't get mad because I know you are trying to help me." The chief psychiatrist handed her a mirror. "Look at yourself. In the last 20 minutes you have become so filled with rage and anger that your chin and neck have broken out in an ugly red rash. Your body betrays the anger which you refuse to feel and express. You cannot go home until you learn to be angry."

After she left the room, the details of her situation were given to us. Early in life, she had developed a pattern of getting what she wanted by being nice. She had a very powerful older sister. To compete was to get smashed, so she cooperated, she compromised, she placated, she became "sweetness and light" personified. She stood ready and willing to do anyone a favor. She waited on her family hand and foot, and she ran her legs off because she was unable to turn down a single request by her church, her children's school or her mother-in-law. Everyone loved her. She had the reputation of a saint. Imagine how her husband must have felt when after 17 years of such a marriage to this person of virtue . . . he came home from work one spring evening to have his beloved try to kill him with an axe.

The psychoanalyst W. R. Bion has helped us to see the way a condition such as this is relevant to the way any of us know our deep inner experiences. He points out that the movement from feeling to thought to expression is inherently frustrating. Our words as we place them on paper are always less than the thought we hold in our minds. The expression of our intuition falls far short of our ideal. We all have experienced the tendency not to say anything if we can't say it "right." Certainly one cannot write without experiencing this tension.

The correlation between expression, thought and the vast, inner world of feeling and emotion is the most difficult of all. The woman in the story had pain but could not suffer it. The pain was not available to her for thought and investigation; she had not discovered her anger. It is, in Bion's phrase, "a thing that is not there."[13] For one in whom restriction and anything less than the ideal are terrifying, the anger and the process by which the anger could be known are intolerable. The anger has been repressed until it is a no-thing. No conjunction exists between the reality, the thought, and the word.

The approach to God, to ultimate reality, to the truth, to the Ground of Being, to the thing-in-itself is no different. The reality lies beyond these words. If there is no conjunction between word and reality, then the reality becomes a thing that is not there. For God to be there we must tolerate the conflict between our ideal self and our real self. The more urgent our need for the ideal, the more difficult is the choice to seek expression and exploration. It takes patient, tolerant, steadfast leadership in order to provide the climate of exploration people need

---

[13]W. R. Bion, *Attention and Interpretation* (London: Tavistock, 1970).

to move into the depths of the spirit and to search self and tradition for appropriate language.

The primary "work" which a patient does in the form of psychotherapy called psychoanalysis is to free associate. This means talking spontaneously and freely about whatever comes to mind. It can be remarkably hard work. There is a tendency to find the right words, to perfect, categorize, judge and interpret one's feelings rather than to simply speak in a direct connection between feeling and expression. Insight and self realization are dependent on letting go and giving oneself permission simply to be. The dynamic is precisely the same in spiritual meditation. One must give up self to find oneself.[14]

An outcome of free association is a correlation between the word expressed and the internal, nonsensual material of emotional space. Memory and desire give way to a trust that it is O.K. to be. The depths of self become known rather than known about. In Bion's words, a new constant conjunction, an at-one-ment, is achieved between word and thought and the ultimate realities of being.

Church leaders need not be experts in philosophical theology or in the details of the church's intellectual history. Church leaders must be able to support moving beyond brick and mortar to the nonsensual side of life, to be guides to assist people in exploring their own meanings. Church leaders must learn to resist the busyness of association and organization so that there is space, time and trust to listen to the still small voice of God.

Leadership in the Shaping of Communitas

A major difficulty for local church leaders is that the very concepts of social system awareness and analysis shift us into metaphors of thought and action tempered by the fires of highly organized institutions and bureaucracies and thus seem alien to the spiritual nature of the church.

---

[14]See Gerald G. May, M. D., *A Spiritual Gift and An Offering in Return: Spiritual Awareness and Western Psychology* (Washington, D. C.: The Alban Institute, 1975).

As discussed earlier, the church includes two different forms of organizational structure, (1) a bureaucratic structure with a differentiated heirarchy of roles and values based upon an employer–employee relationship; and (2) an association structure with members grouped around common goals and with voluntary allegiance and leaders who work for the constituency.

Leaders must be aware of and responsive to both of these aspects of church life. At the same time at the heart of church life is the element of corporate worship, a persisting form of antistructure. Different metaphors must be evoked to help us think about this element of church life and the relation of leadership to it.

To describe this unique religious dimension of the organized life of a congregation, we shall use the term *communitas*. To identify the element of leadership that uniquely relates to communitas, we shall use the word *charisma*.

Communitas is a term adopted from the anthropologist Victor Turner.[15] Turner uses the word to describe a state of society characterized by spontaneity and immediacy. As contrasted with the normal experience of society as differentiated, heirarchical, and structurally segmented, communitas is an unstructured state in which all are equal and yet each is uniquely validated. Communitas is an experience of basic equality and integrity.

It is a situation most likely to be found in transitional situations—perhaps as commonplace as a vacation or as unusual as an ecstatic religious experience. Turner's anthropological study of religious rites of passage led him to see that communitas was the essential feature of these crucial spiritual transitions. Communitas is an experience of standing apart from the usual structures of life, being able to see clearly through myth and ritual the real nature of life as it is normally experienced. In communitas mutuality of belief and mutuality of belonging merge into one. "The great historical religions have, in the course of time, learned how to incorporate enclaves

---

[15]Victor W. Turner, *The Ritual Process* (Chicago: Aldine, 1969).

of communitas within their institutionalized structures—just as tribal religions do with their *rites de passage*—and to oxygenate, so to speak, the mystical body by making provision for those ardent souls who wish to live in communitas and poverty all their lives."[16]

The concept communitas captures some of the unique, sacred, life-transforming qualities of the ritual and sacramental life of the church. The unique quality of leadership that is the nourishment of communitas we have chosen to call charisma. In the New Testament charisma is grace-gift. Charisma is potentially given to every Christian. Love is the greatest grace-gift of all (I Cor. 13). Following the usage of the sociologist Max Weber, charisma has come to commonly stand for the capacity to inspire awe in others and hence to gain their allegiance. In our context, the word bears all of these meanings, standing as a reminder that each person has a gift to inspire in others that connection with the vital, divine, life-determining power of the Spirit that is the force of communitas. In moments of charismatic leadership the individual becomes the realization of his or her own gifts and thus symbolizes for all a life lived to the fullest, connected to the very Ground of Being.

To lead with charisma in the establishment of communitas throughout the gathering and worship of the local church is a mystery not to be grasped by techniques. Both clergy and lay leaders who possess this quality do seem to be serious students of Scripture, hard workers, and pastorally faithful. Leaders with charisma and churches with communitas have authority. There is a sense of stability, clarity, and of firmly rooted faith that permeates the climate of the church. Ultimately these demands come down to the capacity of the leadership to clearly cope with the crises of authenticity described by Fletcher. In the maintenance of the institution, in the forging of consensus, and in the realm of worship and theological exploration, the one element that transcends all else in importance is the continuing

---

[16]Victor W. Turner, "Passages, Margins and Poverty, Religious Symbols of Communitas," *Worship,* vol. 46, no. 8.

testing and resolution of the recurrent crises of authentic ministry.

The management theorist Peter Drucker once compared a manager to an orchestra conductor: Both must create a whole that is greater than the sum of the parts. However, the conductor has the composer's musical score as a guide and hence is only an interpreter, whereas the manager must be both conductor and composer.[17] The manager of ministry is also both conductor and composer. But the music that emerges can't just be beautiful music; it must be music authentically in tune with the celestial.

---

[17]Peter F. Drucker, *The Practice of Management* (New York: Harper & Row, 1954).

6

The Primary Task of Ministry

The occasion was the annual two-day retreat of the clergy of the area. In the usual tradition a guest headline speaker was present to address them. His topic was the work of the ordained ministry today. In a talk on the prophetic role of the clergy, the speaker made the point that the verification of the Christian life takes place in the secular world, not in the sanctuary. He went on to say that the church's task is to then sanctify and redeem the world.

This occurrence is significant because such banal, nonsensical statements are so common in the church. The statement was intended to communicate some information to a group of institutional leaders about their distinctive role in the light of the overall task of the church. But the statement conjured up only frustration and bewilderment. The clergy were looking for guidance, for information to help them relate their tasks as leaders to the overall task or purpose of the church. What they found was the usual empty generalization.

Statements of purpose or mission or task are intended to be guides for action. When any person, group, or organization attempts to be rational about behavior, goals, objectives, and programs, the question of basic purpose is inescapable. The question becomes, "Is what we intend to do consistent with our purpose?" Our intentional actions, every goal or behavior we set for ourselves, are based on a set of assumptions concerning our identity, our basic purpose, and the nature of our situation or environment.

Deciding to move in direction X instead of Y or Z, implies

criteria. Every time people, groups, or organizations sense a problem or concern, they are noticing a gap between the way things are and the way people think they ought to be. It would seem that in every instance an overall purpose underlies the actions taken. However, though purpose is pervasively present, it is also persistently illusory.

Some organizational theorists suggest that organizational purpose is an unresolvable question. Standing in the way of even a rudimentary answer is the complexity of the issue and the lack of adequate, valid data. Perhaps the concept of purpose itself is an impediment to facing the complex actualities of organizational life. "Might it be that any organization cannot or does not have purpose of its own, but that its purpose is formed by both internal and external forces—a dynamic concordance of internal and external power forces?"[1]

One test of this statement is to examine the planning guides and procedures used by congregations. Commonly the procedures begin with some assessment of needs. While there may be Bible-study sessions or reflection periods built into the planning process to "get in touch" with the basic purposes of the church, the task of planning usually begins with gathering information as to the wants, needs, and aspirations of the membership and the community. The examination of the purpose of church and parish is done more by implication than by specific investigation, and our first-hand experience at assisting congregations to clarify their fundamental objectives substantiated this approach. Very little direct investigation can be done without foundering in social conflict or losing the way in complexity.

A recent article in a church newspaper is an example of the entanglements that can arise. The article quoted a group of Anglican and Roman Catholic theologians as stating that "the church is not a man-made society of likeminded people who are trying to live Christian lives and to exert some kind of Christian influence upon the world. Rather it is a community created and

---

[1]John A. Beckett, *Management Dynamics: The New Synthesis* (New York: McGraw-Hill, 1971).

called by God whose task is evangelisation and salvation."[2] The statement seems to say that God has given us the basic purpose of the church if we will only take note of the answer. To this we respond, "Yes, but it is still human beings who must receive, interpret, and respond to God's directive." This entangling briar patch of issues is where discussions of the purpose of the church seem to begin and end.

Avery Dulles, a Roman Catholic Theologian, has delineated five distinct models of the church present in theology and practice.[3] They are, in effect, five quite different ways of understanding the basic identity and mission of the church. Dulles demonstrates the way each model of the church differs along such dimensions as:

1. What are the ties that hold the church members together? What constitutes the bonds of union?

2. Who are the recipients of the gifts that the church has to bestow? Who are the beneficiaries?

3. What is the purpose of the benefits? What is it that people receive or are enabled to do because of the church?

4. What is the primary nature of church work? What is the dominant form of ministry by those who have been ordained?

5. What is the stance toward revelation? How does the church understand the nature of God's self-disclosure?

Table E summarizes the five models and the functional differences between them. One of Dulles' major points is that the Church as a whole has been rocked by a series of rapid shifts in its ruling paradigm or prevailing model. Because each model has its own set of accompanying values, images, and priorities the end result of these rapid changes has been to remove the ground of common meanings and commitments. His book helps us to see the complexity of discerning and agreeing on the

[2]"The Virginia Churchman," vol. 84, no. 7, December 1975.
[3]Avery Dulles, *Models of the Church* (New York: Doubleday, 1974).

TABLE E

Model	Bonds of Union	Who Are the Beneficiaries	Purpose of the Benefits	Dominant Form of Ministry	Stance Toward Revelation
Institutional	The visible tests of membership in the profession of doctrine; regular worship and obedience to ecclesiastical authority.	The visible, juridical membership, that is, those who belong.	Eternal life—"He cannot have God for his Father who does not have the Church for his Mother" (Cyprian).	The priestly "power of the keys" to confer what is needed for salvation.	Objective and complete. The church is the guardian and conserver of the truth, which it holds and transmits.
Mystical Communion	The gifts of the Holy Spirit in a transforming mystical communion.	The members (but can be an invisible membership); those animated by faith.	To lead people into communion with God.	To develop the church as a living form of community.	Subjective—emotional grace at work in the soul of every believer; the church as the gathering of fellow recipients.
Sacramental	The social visible signs of grace operative in believing Christians.	All those who are better able to live their faith due to contact with the believing, loving church.	To strengthen members' response to the grace of God.	Eucharistic celebration.	Two-leveled: (1) implicit (interior invisible); (2) explicit (exterior symbolic). Ongoing. Church as symbol.

Herald	Faith—as a response to proclamation of the Christ event.	Those who hear the Lord and respond in Faith.	To proclaim the message; to evangelize.	Proclamation.	Complete revelation as the word of God in Bible and sermon.
Servant	Mutual brotherhood in those who serve together.	All who need and receive help.	To be of help to all humanity; to keep alive the hopes of people for the Kingdom of God.	To point out the dangers of dehumanization and to inspire concrete actions to transform society.	Ongoing—viewed as analogous to an evolutionary force in creation; Christ an immediate leap forward.

functional implications of a theological symbol such as salvation or evangelism. We can see, for instance, how either concept is directly related to the actual congregational response to the questions listed above. Thus the pastor who understands salvation as healing may turn to counseling as the dominant form of ministry to the despairing, psychically crippled who come seeking health. Or for pastors who believe that salvation is the promise of eternal life and that there is no salvation outside the church, a concern for the institution and its membership logically becomes the dominant form of ministry. Dulles' historical analysis makes it evident that there is no single form to the basic identity of the church; even within one tradition many aspects must be examined for a clear picture of the church's nature to emerge.

These inherently competing views of basic purpose are present in most congregations as well as in scholarly theological writing. It is small wonder that congregational planning practices infer rather than delineate the mission of the church. Nor is the issue as simple as clarifying the ideal purpose of the church among differing views. The constraints imposed by the environment; the differing goals of the members; the multiple, hidden, unanticipated outcomes so usual in organizational life make stated purposes, even when clear, far from accurate descriptions of the actual functioning of the local church.

However much our usual common-sense approach tells us to begin by clarifying purpose and then correcting wanderings, most social-system theorists see this approach as a dead-end street. "The essential difficulty with this purposive or design approach is that an organization characteristically includes more and less than is indicated by the design of its founder or the purpose of its leader. Some of the factors assumed in the design may be lacking or so distorted in operational practice as to be meaningless, while unforeseen embellishments dominate the organizational structure."[4] In the struggle to unravel the ministry of the church, is there a way to look at purpose or mission that offers a way out of this thicket?

---

[4]Daniel Katz and Robert L. Kahn, *The Social Psychology of Organizations* (New York: Wiley, 1966).

The Functional Approach to Purpose

Every organization performs a wide variety of tasks or functions. In systems language an organization is a patterned set of activities taking in energy (people, money, knowledge) from the environment and transforming that energy into outputs such as products or services. Each function is an energic input–transformation–output process. Each function is involved with the relationship between systems; the organization is always a subsystem of a larger system or environment. Thus in systems terms purpose has to do with intended relationships between systems. For the church purpose can only be the result of the interaction of congregation and environment. For this reason A. K. Rice, a prominent systems theorist, chooses to use the concept of primary task rather than ideas such as purpose or mission.[5] Primary task is the task the organization must perform to survive in a given environment at a given time.

Statements of congregational purpose are only ideas in the minds of their creators. A congregational purpose or goal represents a rationalized, hoped-for achievement. In contrast, the phrase *primary task* points to the actual transaction between the enterprise and its environment. When we examine a live organization, what we notice is that it receives materials, services, energy—a variety of inputs—from its environment, transforms these inputs in some fashion, and then exports the finished product or service back into the environment. The dominant input–conversion–export process is the primary task—the actual mission being performed, as seen in the diagram below:

Input:		Output:
Original State	→ Transformation →	Altered State

All three dimensions must be examined for the task to be described. This may not seem important in theory, but in practice it is a crucial and useful distinction that represents another

---

[5]A. K. Rice, *The Enterprise and its Environment* (London: Tavistock, 1963), p. 17.

advantage the concept of primary task holds over statements of purpose. Purpose statements are generally static. At best they touch only the output, or the transforming aspects, of the church's life.

Clergy continually lament the inability of the church to carry out its mission because its own members are not converted, convicted Christians. Purpose statements that reflect only the output side of the institution (to provide a faithful witness to Christ) are partly responsible for this despair because they incorrectly shape expectations and perceptions. In fact, the church is always in the business of converting sinners into redeemed souls, of transforming souls longing for golden idols into spirits set free in Christ. This living quality of from what, by what, to what is necessary for clarity of ministry. The concept of primary task helps remind us that in this world the task of each of us is never complete. We are pilgrims on the road, both individually and collectively—a reality that must be incorporated into our thought and practice in regard to the mission and ministry of the church.

Another practical advantage of the concept of primary task is that it keeps reminding us that the activities of the church are not ends in themselves. Fellowship or worship or education or counseling are at their best means of grace; that is, they are vehicles through which people can alter their lives. Listen to your own leadership group for a while and see how easy it is to focus all energy on the means and forget the reason why. Is this trip really necessary? Do we have to give up time for prayer and meditation, obliterate family time, and strong-arm neighborhood participation away from other community involvements in order to make the new church program go? It is genuinely difficult amidst the realities of congregational life to remember that the outcome we seek is not more and better activity but people made able to love God, self and neighbor. One of the most prevalent disabling problems of church life is the tendency to reach out to people by increasing their sense of obligation rather than by responding to their need.

Recent conversations with two church leaders about the coming year and the scope of their work revealed striking contrasts in their focus. Most of the first conversation focused on issues such as the parish planning process, the upcoming stewardship campaign, and increasing the rate of member participation. In short, the focus was entirely upon the systems of the congregation, as if the pastor's job was solely to manage the internal affairs of a congregation.

The second conversation focused upon a series of changes in the city school system and their impact on the community and thus the parish school; several specific, family situations and the variety of ways the church was attempting to support them through some crisis periods; and the ways in which the church was making its ministry known to the community.

The second leader seemed to be standing on the cutting edge of the church. She was looking at the needs of the city—the inputs to the congregation—and the actual impact the church was having upon people—the outputs of the congregation. The second leader, in line with the concept of primary task, was considering needs, the capacity to respond to the needs, and the resulting changes in the original needful individuals and settings. The tasks the enterprise is performing involve all three functions. It is only our own cloudy vision that allows us to forget that these are the basic, organic functions of any enterprise or system.

All congregations perform many tasks. Discerning the tasks that are faithful to the demands of both the Gospel and human need is quite difficult. Are any one or two tasks clearly dominant in the planning of the leadership or the functioning of the congregation? Is there any correspondence between intent and operation? If leaders are to concern themselves with purpose, then they must examine the dominant functions of the system—the primary tasks with which the church is engaged—the nature of the inputs from the environment, the transformations that occur, and the actual outputs. This process of functional analysis is practical and far reaching in its consequences. It does not imply that people and organizations are without purpose; that they do not change their behavior as conditions change in order to move closer to a goal. It does mean that very often an organization's stated purpose is radically different from the actual behavior it exhibits. The purposeful direction of a local church is shaped by many forces, more extensive and intensive than the will of the leadership.

For I do not the good I want, but the evil I do not want is what I do. Now if I do what I do not want, it is no longer I that do it, but sin which dwells within me. (Romans 7:19–20, RSV).

The principalities and powers inherent in institutional life do not yield to an easy, rational discussion of the good we intend. In fact, these same powers usually land such discussions in a cloud of confusion. The energy is better used in facing the reality of the church's current functioning with the world about it. In the dominant or primary tasks may be discovered the present purposive activity of the congregation.

We would argue that the primary task is the best place to begin to look at the basic purpose or ministry and mission of the church and to keep subordinate matters subordinate. It means that the mission of a congregation is discovered in its relation to the community. Let's look again at what primary task implies for a congregation. A basic organizational system as depicted by two management theorists Kast and Rosenzweig[6] is shown in the following diagram:

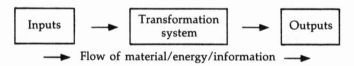

This organizational model reminds us that an enterprise exists by continually interacting with its environment. It is obvious that the survival of a biological system is dependent upon this interchange with the environment; what may not be quite so obvious is that an organization or congregation is no different. A staff debate over whether or not to initiate a new worship service using an innovative, contemporary liturgy is punctuated by such comments as, "I think there really is a

---

[6]Fremont E. Kast and James E. Rosenzweig, *Organization and Management* (New York: McGraw-Hill, 1970).

congregation to be formed around this service," which recognize that the survival of the new service is a function of its interaction with elements in the community. A congregation survives, grows, ministers by taking in people from the community; acting upon them through activities such as worship, education, and fellowship; and then sending them out to act upon the community and finally to return again to the congregational setting. Of the many, many functions a local church carries out, which are dominant? What are the specific inputs? What means are utilized for transformation? To what ends do they lead?

It is not surprising that the typical pastor or congregational leader is inexperienced in answering these questions. The input side of church life—the hungers, wants, and needs of individuals and of communities, as well as their strengths and resources —represents areas of life defined in our culture primarily by the behavioral sciences. The output side of church life—the exploration and explanation of the nature of life in Christ—has been and still remains the province of theological and Biblical studies. The transforming aspect of church life has been addressed for the most part by pastoral or practical theology. Unfortunately, this intellectual separation is not allowed the pastor; the actual functioning of a congregation comprises all three aspects together. If pastors wish to be disciplined and thoughtful in the execution of ministry, they must integrate in their own minds and hearts what has been separate in their study and training.

In our context input is basic human religious needs. Many statements of such need exist:

Religion can be seen as a general rationalizer for all those inescapable contradictions of expectation and experience with which even the best of all possible worlds must confront its most trusting traveler. . . . Religious belief and practice always originate in situations of social and cultural stress and are, in fact, an effort on the part of the stress-laden to construct systems of dogma, myth and ritual which are internally coherent as well as true descriptions of a world system and which thus will serve as guides to efficient action. . . . But religion does not offer just any solution: Characteristically, it offers a solution that assures the believer that life and organization will win, that

*death and disorganization will lose, in their struggle to become the characteris-
tic condition of self and cosmos.* [7]

*Self awareness, reason and imagination have disrupted the harmony
which characterizes animal existence. Their emergence has made man into an
anomaly, into a freak of the universe. . . . Cast into his world at an accidental
place and time, he is forced out of it, again accidentally. Being aware of
himself, he realizes his powerlessness and the limitations of his existence. He
visualizes his own end: Death. . . . The disharmony of man's existence
generates needs which far transcend those of his animal origin. These needs
result in an imperative drive to restore a unity and equilibrium between
himself and the rest of nature. . . . Devotion to an aim, or an idea, or a power
transcending man such as God, is an expression of this need for completeness
in the process of living. . . . There is no one without a religious need, a need
to have a frame of orientation and an object of devotion. . . .* [8]

*At their creative best, religions retrace our earliest inner experiences,
giving tangible form to vague evils, and reaching back to the earliest individual
sources of trust; at the same time, they keep alive the common symbols of
integrity distilled by the generations.* [9]

*The parental faith which supports the trust emerging in the newborn
has throughout history sought its institutional safeguard (and on occasion,
found its greatest enemy) in organized religion. Trust born of care is, in fact,
the touchstone of the actuality of a given religion. All religions have in common
the periodical, childlike surrender to a Provider or providers, who dispense
earthly fortune as well as spiritual health; some demonstration of man's
smallness by way of reduced posture and humble gesture; the admission in
prayer and song of misdeeds, of misthoughts, and of evil intentions; fervent
appeal for inner unification by divine guidance; and finally, the insight that
individual trust must become a common faith, individual mistrust a commonly
formulated evil, while the individual's restoration must become part of the
ritual practice of many and must become a sign of trustworthiness in the
community.* [10]

---

[7]Anthony F. C. Wallace, *Religion: An Anthropological View* (New York:
Random House, 1966), pp. 29–30.
[8]Erich Fromm, *Psychoanalysis and Religion* (New York: Bantam Books,
1967), pp. 22–25.
[9]Erik H. Ericson, *Young Man Luther* (New York: Norton, 1962), p. 264.
[10]Erik H. Ericson, *Childhood and Society,* (New York: Norton, 1963), p.
250.

We have to look for the answer to the problem of freedom where it is most absent: in the transference, the fatal and crushing enslaver of men. The transference fetishizes mystery, terror and power; it holds the self bound in its grip. Religion answers directly to the problem of transference by expanding awe and terror to the cosmos where they belong. It also takes the problem of self-justification and removes it from the objects near at hand. We no longer have to please those around us, but the very source of creation—the powers that created us, not those into whose lives we accidentally fell. Our life ceases to be a reflexive dialogue with the standards of our wives, husbands, friends and leaders, and becomes instead measured by standards of the highest heroism, ideals truly fit to lead us on and beyond ourselves. In this way we fill ourselves with independent values, can make free decisions, and, most importantly, can lean on powers that really support us and do not oppose us. [11]

Lord, let me know mine end, and the number of my days; that I may be certified how long I have to live; Behold, thou hast made my days as it were a span long, and mine age is even as nothing in respect of thee; and verily every man living is altogether vanity. For man walketh in a vain shadow, and disquieteth himself in vain; he heapeth up riches, and cannot tell who shall gather them. And now, Lord, what is my hope? Truly my hope is even in thee. Deliver me from all mine offences; and make me not a rebuke unto the foolish (Psalm 39:4–8, KJV).

I should utterly have fainted, but that I believe verily to see the goodness of the Lord in the land of the living. O tarry thou the Lord's leisure; be strong, and he shall comfort thine heart; and put thou thy trust in the Lord (Psalm 27:13–14, KJV).

Good preachers have always known that their sermons must be addressed to the situation of the listener. These concepts of the human situation describe the human dilemma to which we are called to respond. Both church leaders and critics of the church have tended to confuse the need with the answer, but explanations of the need do not furnish the answer. We need not be frightened of the functional language of psychology and anthropology as it seeks to unfold some small measure of the human condition. Our real concern is the qual-

---

[11]Ernest Becker, *The Denial of Death* (New York: The Free Press, 1973), p. 202.

ity and transforming power of the answer that we present.

But here we should note that the very concepts of function and transformation are quite new for the church. Within the understanding of the church as contained in Dulles' herald and institutional models, the question of human need is assumed by the answer. Revelation is static; visible membership in the church confers all that is necessary, so why worry about the deep dilemmas of human existence? Whether that membership is the response in an altar call to the proclamation of the Word or is obedience to ecclesiastical authority, the functional relationship between spiritual need and Christian answer goes unexamined. And indeed for much of Christian history, there has seemed little need to examine this correlation. For most of our history in the Western world, people became Christian primarily through the forces of political action and cultural socialization not through personal choice. It is still true that a great many people enter the church largely through the forces of socialization and accomodation.[12]

Where people turn to the church because it is what people normally do, or because it is a happy accomodation to the pressures of new relationships and friends, nothing forces the church to examine the interface between need and response. When you've got the only game in town, you don't usually think about what is causing the customer to play. It is enough that we own the game.

When Reuel Howe first popularized Tillich's principle of correlation in *Man's Need and God's Action,*[13] he received severe criticism for the title and was told that he should reverse the terms. It is enough that man be obedient to God's command. That tension is still with us today. Nevertheless, everywhere we look in our culture, we see evidence that both young and old are involved in a searching religious quest. The decline in the church's influence and membership is certainly not due to a decline in the religious need of modern, secular men and

---

[12]R. W. Bibby and M. B. Brinkerhoff, "Sources of Religious Involvement: Issues for Future Empirical Investigation," *Review of Religious Research,* vol. 15, no. 2, Winter 1974.

[13](Greenwich: The Seabury Press, 1953).

women. The nonauthoritarian, fragmented nature of our culture presents people with a bewildering array of religious
groups, value systems, and ways to self-enlightenment. If we
suffer from the supermarket, impulse-shopper orientation to
these offerings, the hunger keeps returning. By identifying
God's answer with church membership, we have become insensitive to the inability of an all-too-human institution to respond to the human religious quest.

When we view the church as a system, the primary input
is the world's religious need. What these authorities cited are
saying is that people everywhere seem to manifest some common themes in their religious quest: The needs to overcome the
contradictions of life and death; cope with disparity and separation; belong to a greater community; and find a sense of security, trust, and integrated meaning. These are the qualities of
life that seem missing, that cause people to turn their faces
toward God and God's house. These needs go very deep within
us. Our religious hungers will not be assuaged by the acquisition of knowledge or by regular performance of prescribed institutional duties.

Let us look at this need more closely using Ericson's phrase
"at their creative best, religious retrace our earliest inner experiences" as the initial clue. Psychoanalysts such as Margaret
Mahler and D. W. Winnicott have been painstakingly investi-
gating the process by which human beings come to self-awareness. Our biological birth and our psychological birth are not
coincident in time. The sense of self as separate from and yet
related to the world, and in particular related to one's own
body, is the result of a slow, unfolding process that only begins
with our biological birth. Mahler calls this the process of separation and individuation.[14]

This earliest and most basic of human struggles takes place
as the infant achieves the capacity to function apart from its
mother, but with an internalized sense of her emotional availability. This struggle can be recognized in a scene familiar to all
of us. Remember or observe anew the reactions of the toddler

---

[14]Margaret S. Mahler, Fred Pine, and Anne Bergman, *The Psychological
Birth of the Human Infant* (New York: Basic Books, 1975).

—the two- to three-year-old—playing in its mother's presence, what happens when she leaves the room and then later reappears. The range of behaviors upon the mother's departure, during her absence, and upon her return are outward manifestations of the child's attempt to achieve a stable self-identity apart from its mother. In these processes are shaped the initial patterns of our capacity to feel loved apart from the lover, to live with the frustration of our needs, and to reconcile both the good and bad found in all those whom we would hope to trust and love. It is upon this foundation that we begin to build the capacity to enter the mutuality of a love relationship that transcends relationships that endure only as long as they are satisfying. In the struggle of separation, in the achievement of individuation, the toddling infant knows for the first time the paradox of what Becker calls "individuality within finitude".

We will never escape this dilemma. It is the awareness of our uniqueness and the awareness of our mortality. It is as Becker says, this synthesis of soul and body that, in Kierkegaard's words, means we cannot flee from dread. Our individuality leaves each of us with the dread of total separation, of ultimate extinction. The dynamic patterns of that first achievement of a sense of separation from mother is the precursor of all future separations from that which gives hope, meaning, and trust to life.

In this context we can see that the language of faith is deeply expressive. To find new life and to be born again, to abide in the Father's love are phrases meant to move us toward the ever more fundamental issues of life. We can see in the Biblical concept of adoption the promise of being able to work through anew the dilemmas made known to us in our first birth as individual selves.

The situation we have described is of an individual dimly aware of a longing to be in community, to achieve a sense of purpose that overshadows the contradictions of our existence —to find an eternally dependable grounding of life. The longing is vague and dim because its well-spring goes to the very core of one's self-birth. The longing, hence its response, is churned and confused because the individual is in a society awash with contradictory, partial answers to our deepest needs.

Our culture bears no unifying myth capable of orienting people and directing them toward freeing answers. The individual's own capacity to work with the nonpragmatic, nonsensual stuff of myth and symbol has been numbed until it is almost nonexistent. Bombarded by the sensory overload of our multimedia world, the individual has learned to perceive only that which seems immediately important; as the capacity for inner symbolic realization has dimmed, so has the power to perceive and to make use of the symbols necessary to carry the richest and deepest human meanings. This is the human condition, the basic input that the church must transform with a new state of being.

We should now begin to see that the demand the world makes upon the church has some prevailing theme. The basic human religious urge seeks security, an all-accepting community, an unfailing pastor, and a religion responsive to human needs. In short, as Jesus and the prophets tried to help us see, the primary and recurrent religious urgency is for comfort, not challenge. It is to find a pastor, a congregation, a God who will overcome the contradictions of our living and dying. There is an initial and recurrent urge for "childlike surrender" to the perfect Provider. As Becker has put it, everyone needs a beyond, but most people play it safe choosing popular, near-at-hand transference objects, earning their immortality in the way their culture dictates—"in the beyonds of others and not their own."

Once individuals are drawn into contact with a congregation, the burden upon congregation and pastor is to convert their need into faith in Christ. At their worst congregations meet this input with the equally erroneous poles of: (1) hard rejection—Only those who already have the courage are welcome here. All piety is scorned. At all times, in all places one must be willing to witness via social action to Christ's concern for the poor and oppressed—or (2) easy acceptance—All piety and religion welcome here. Be loyal, and life will be O.K. Lay ministry means serving the institution.

For most of us the comfortable pew can seem pretty welcome; perhaps none of us ever leave it permanently behind. Each new age, stage, and circumstance may surface once again the wish to find elsewhere what seems so grievously lost within ourselves. The door of a congregation must open easily when people knock, but the path on the other side must be narrow and straight. A recent extensive professional attitude survey of a large urban congregation showed the great majority of the members stating that the business of the church is religion. They are right if we consider only the entrance–input view of congregational life. As we shall see, however, the business of transformation and output are quite different.

The single most helpful clue for us in clarifying the primary task has been the work of the Grubb Institute in England.[15] Bruce Reed and Barry Palmer of the institute describe the basic religious quest as a search for a dependable relationship. Everyday life is not dependable. When our store of courage is used up, we become restless until we find our rest with God. The authors picture life as a process of oscillation—we move back and forth from the structured, rational world of work to the statusless, childlike surrender of worship. The church is the institution that allows this regression to dependence to occur in regular and controlled ways for the benefit of the whole of society. Utilizing the input–transformation–output model, Reed and Palmer depict the primary task of the church as shown in Figure 4.[16] The oscillation is a recurring movement from society to dependence on a person or object

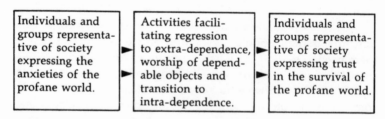

Figure 4. The Primary Task of the Church, Using the Input-Transformation-Output Model.

---

[15]See *Action Information,* vol. 1, no. 3, September, 1975, (Alban Institute) for a report of a conference summarizing Grubb theory.
[16]Bruce Reed and Barry Palmer, *The Local Church and its Environment* (Washington D.C.: Alban Institute, 1975).

outside of self (extra-dependence) to a renewed inner strength (intra-dependence) to a vitalized work and life in society. When the church contains this oscillation and keeps people dependent rather than sending them out to express their faith in the world, then it has distorted its primary task. The frequency and extent of our own oscillating movement vary as circumstances change.

The Grubb theorists are illuminating a process that in more traditional terms is the nature of faith development. Our conviction is that the process of faith development ought to be the actual primary task of the church. We believe that faith development is a task obedient to the will of God and the needs of this world, a primary task that clarifies the nature of lay ministry and ordained ministry.

Faith is the stance from which we interpret and respond to experience. Tillich speaks of the presence of faith as the courage to be; Ericson speaks of a basic trust in life, a trust born of care. We see such concepts as the stance of faith. The theologian and researcher James Fowler says that faith is "the response to one's sense of relatedness to the ultimate conditions and depths of existence."[17] Faith development has to do with the response of the total self to the boundary conditions of life—death, crisis, and awesome ecstasy. Faith and belief are two different matters, although belief is an important ingredient in faith.[18] Belief is commonly understood as rational assent to the official doctrine and dogma of the church. Such belief can give order, structure, and meaning to life. However, the identification of belief with faith is a source of confusion to many Christians. They feel a deep and abiding trust in God but find themselves dissenting from parts of what they perceive to be the institution's belief system. They notice that each segment of the institution seems to have its own official set of beliefs and that they are subject to revisions by theological interpretation. They perceive quite readily that belief is a form of indoctrination.

---

[17]James W. Fowler, III, "Toward a Developmental Perspective on Faith," *Religious Education,* March–April 1974.
[18]See Thomas Luckmann, "Belief, Unbelief and Religion," in *The Culture of Unbelief,* ed. Rocco Caporale and Antonio Grumelli. (Berkeley: University of California Press, 1971).

Faith on the other hand, transcends rational assent and is the organic response of the individual to the conditions of life. The content of faith in Christ is a spirit renewed in mind and body.

It is easier to recognize faith than to describe it. After the 1976 Democratic National Convention, *The Washington Post,* in a front-page article, described Martin Luther King, Sr.'s benediction at the convention's close. Haynes Johnson, the author of the article, pointed out that what King said was not as important as his saying it at that moment and place. "Here he was, a man who has suffered as much grief as anyone should have to endure—his son, Martin, assassinated, his wife insanely murdered while playing 'The Lord's Prayer' on the church organ, his youngest son drowning in his swimming pool—an old black man from the Deep South preaching about reconciliation and faith and love."[19] Faith is not the equivalent of a static knowledge in or belief about a set of values or a creedal statement. Many of the Psalms are expressions of faith:

Even though I walk through the valley of the shadow of death, I fear no evil; for thou art with me; thy rod and thy staff they comfort me (Psalm 23:4, RSV).

I lift up my eyes to the hills. From whence does my help come? My help comes from the Lord, who made heaven and earth (Psalm 121:1–2, RSV).

Luther said that the Psalter is "a fine, clear, pure mirror which will show you what Christianity really is."[20] Not only do the Psalms give us a picture of the faith, they also provide for us the path of faith development. The Psalms are most human documents of sorrow, fear, joy, and hope. They are records of the deep inner emotions of people of profound faith.

Erich Fromm has pointed out that a number of the Psalms (such as Psalms 6, 8, 22, 90) mirror deep and dramatic changes of mood within the author.[21] Fromm calls these dynamic

---

[19]Haynes Johnson, "After Speeches, True Drama," *The Washington Post* July 17, 1976.

[20]Quoted in Arthur Weiser, *The Psalms, A Commentary* (Philadelphia: Westminster, 1962).

[21]Erich Fromm, *You Shall Be As Gods* (New York: Holt, Rinehart & Winston, 1966).

Psalms to express the fact they are pictures of a transforming process, a process of movement from despair to hope. Psalm 6 is a good example. It begins with an expression of fear and hope in verses 1–3; then in verses 4 and 5 the hope becomes an appeal to God—"Turn, O Lord, save my life." In verses 6 and 7 the emotion has become a cry of deep and utter despair, and all hope has fled: "I am weary with my mourning." Suddenly in verses 8, 9, and 10 the psalmist proclaims, "Depart from me, all you workers of evil; for the Lord has heard the sound of my weeping." An inner transformation has occurred as the psalmist moves into and through the full experience of his situation. This trust that God has answered has come as the writer has touched the depths of his own despair.

The Psalms give us a picture of the development of faith. The task of faith development can now be translated into the elements and processes of congregational life. The dynamic movement of the Psalms helps us to see that the supporting role of the congregation is to provide the security for a movement through the pain of life. The development of a genuine sense of trust in a loving and supportive community in the church is, we believe, a prerequisite for the development of faith. For most Americans the path is too perilous if there are not guides, companions, and those who have gone before clustered about us. At the same time community within the congregation cannot be an end in itself. The plight of the burned-out, exhausted volunteer is common in the American church. It seems to us to be a symptom of the search for God being subverted by the idealization of congregational fellowship and belonging. The liturgical phrase, "Go in peace; the mass is ended," is a fitting reminder that the church is not doing its job unless the outcome of life in the church is the capacity to go in peace into the world. As one congregation has put it, "We see the church as a basic training camp for the battle of life, not as a front-line combat unit."

Any local church discussion of its mission today occurs against the ever present backdrop of the large-scale social involvement of the 1960s. Anyone who has had any exposure at all to such discussion knows how warm still are the fires generated by the bold venture of the church into the arena of social action. What we have learned is similar to the findings of Jeffrey Hadden and Charles Longino, Jr.[22]

First, the liberal denominations came close to losing sight of their associational, voluntary character and considered their mission solely from the standpoint of theological values and ideals. The primary task of the church is to bring together human need and divine grace. To be aware of a prevailing need for the comfortable pew, for the relaxation of dependent faith, does not mean the church must content itself with the answer of cheap grace. As Hadden and Longino write, "Rather the task is to communicate [to church members] the structural and ideological bases of our continuing cultural turmoil, to convince them that intentional morality is not enough, and, beyond this to help them develop the faith and courage to participate in the creation of a new social order." Like the tension in the sacraments, the church holds in tension the earthly elements of human need and the transcendent power of God's grace. In the tension of this correlation our mission is forged.

Our own restatement of the task of faith development as it occurs in the local congregation is diagramed in Figure 5.

In American culture the decision to join the church comes from a variety of sources. Family customs, the influence of a neighborhood social circle, the hope of moving up the socioeconomic ladder: these and many factors contribute to that initial choice to enter the door of one of the many churches dotting the American landscape. Once in the door every individual makes a second decision, whether or not to stay and actually belong to the church of choice. This is a period of testing, a period in which the individual is learning the ropes, feeling the way into a new group of persons, finding out their values and ways of accepting and responding to a newcomer. The individual's hope for security and meaning begin to be invested in the pastor or the worship service or some circle of church friends. The new member is dependent for faith upon those about him. The individual is transferring needs for security, dependability, and the search for a foundation to life onto

---

[22]Jeffrey K. Hadden and Charles F. Longino, Jr., *Gideon's Gang—A Case Study of the Church in Social Action* (Philadelphia: Pilgrim Press, 1974).

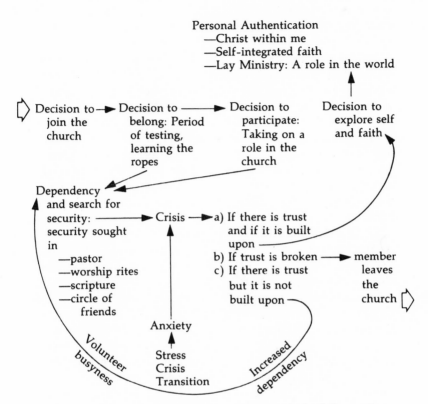

Personal Authentication
—Christ within me
—Self-integrated faith
—Lay Ministry: A role in the world

Figure 5. Task of Faith Development as It Occurs in the Local Congregation.

the pastor or some central aspect of the church's life. If these conditions of fellowship and dependability are met, the new member is likely to make still another decision—the decision to participate. Now the individual becomes active in the church, giving volunteer energy, committing financial resources, taking on his or her own unique role in the life of the congregation. Faith is still dependent upon others, and indeed the member may lean even more heavily on others for personal strength and security as he becomes an active and accepted part of a congregation. Life, however, is never stable, nor congregations and pastors without their disappointing features. A change in life circumstances, the aging process, illness, the death of a loved one, these life crises and transitions bring stress into one's life.

This anxiety will now put the church to the test. The resultant anxiety is brought into the congregation by the member. If trust is present, the anxiety is noticed and built upon. The member is helped to move into the pain and stress of his or her condition and to make the decision to explore self and faith. If the trust is broken, if the individual perceives that the anxiety finds no meaningful response, a direction is started that usually ends in the individual slowly withdrawing from church life and finally dropping out altogether. A third possibility is that the congregation responds in a trusting and caring fashion but that this support, rather than strengthening the individual's own faith, becomes focused instead in an even tighter and stronger dependency upon pastor and congregation to provide the strength and life the individual feels is missing. This response takes church life and involvement as a panacea for life's dilemmas and ultimately, we believe, leads to an idolatry of pastor and church. At its best the church provides the security for a movement through the pain of life to a personal realization of the inheritance of the kingdom of heaven, to a faith that provides the courage for working for a world in which love and justice prevail. None of us, of course, sustain this life of faith for long without having to turn to our community for support. Nevertheless, as the diagram indicates, we see a very real difference between the response which leads to greater dependency on the church and the response which leads to a realized lay ministry in the world. It is our belief that each new stage of life forces a person to move again through this cycle of faith.

Mission, or primary task, is one of the four elements of the ministry system. The church as a whole has historically comprised and mixed together at least five quite different understandings of its core mission. Extensive experience, with a variety of groups, of Dulles' five models of the church dramatically illustrates church members' confusing the conflicting understandings of the church. One man expressed the sense of clarity and relief he felt when the Dulles model helped him to see a map that at least explained many of the present disputes over the role of the church: "Perhaps I'm unusual, but for the first time I could understand why our discussions of lay ministry and evangelism lead to so little clarification. We all seem to have such mixed understandings of what we are basically about."

Congregational lists of program goals do little to clarify the core mission or primary task of the church. The actual ongoing life of a church—its interaction with the community and interactions among the members generate an identity or character that transcends any rational scheme of planning. Social conflict, threatened or actual, makes the process of mission identification an area often avoided or smoothed over. The concept of primary task is a way of looking at a congregation's answer to the question of human need and God's action. Primary task demands both theological clarification and organizational analysis for the church to identify both its intended mission and its actual functional mission.

The primary task of the church is faith development. It is to move from a faith dependent upon others through a process of personal search and exploration to a faith that is owned—integral to self identity and freely chosen personal values. (see Figure 5). The church fails when it exists only to build itself as an institution. Fellowship is not an end in itself but rather a vehicle that people might see the world as it is and live in that world with justice and love. The church is a setting in which by the grace of God people may constantly renew their basic trust in life. The test of our capacity to be such a setting lies in the quality of the society in which we live.

7

The Community and the Management of Ministry

In the preceeding chapters, we have defined and analyzed ministry as a system. We have seen it as a dynamic process of interrelating a community—an organized congregation of Christian people, the purpose around which the people have gathered, and the leaders who have been set apart by the group with the special role of facilitating and managing the process. Next we will discuss how the four core components of ministry can be related. Based upon our observations of parishes in a variety of settings, we will share our perceptions of the management styles and strategies that issue in effective ministry. Our purpose in this chapter is to suggest a model for managing the basic relationship between a church and its community. This relationship is only one of the necessary interactions, and a first step in managing ministry, but the quality of the other relationships depends upon the character and depth of this one.

In Chapter 3 we presented the community as a primary component in the ministry system. We looked at the indivisible relationship between community and church, and offered a framework in which each church can define its particular community. We saw also the complex of community trends and processes that influence and interact with processes internal to the church, giving both the community and the church their unique existence. Finally, we saw the dynamic and parallel life cycles of communities and the churches that serve them. Churches whose growth and change patterns are synchronized with those of their communities are able to serve with purpose in each successive stage.

We now turn our attention to assisting the leaders of Christian congregations to recognize the reality of the community–church connection, to define the church's parish area appropriately, to understand the distinctive characteristics of their community, and to continuously challenge the congregation as it plans and programs to test for "goodness of fit" between community needs and the church's offering. Within the framework of community–church relationships that has been discussed, we can consider the task of planning and programing for extending the church's ministry.

The Management of Planning

To plan is to systematically relate the purpose of a group to the context in which it functions, to the opportunities and limitations of a time span, and to a range of strategies through which its task can be achieved. It is a process of understanding and preparation.

The purpose of the church is to be the people of God—a communion of saints, a "called-out" people—in the community. They are the "light of the world," the "salt of the earth," the "leaven of society." They are the few who symbolize and reflect God's working throughout the community. The purpose of the church is different from that of some other community groups, it is different primarily in that the church is called to *be* rather than to *do*.

The political party, historical society, and civic club, for example, are formed to do or accomplish something—elect their candidates, preserve the community's heritage, or urge citizen participation in government. The church, however, is people (many of the same people who are members of the other groups) in whose lives God has acted and continues to act. As the church they have no product to sell or cause to support. God is the actor; they have only to be his people.

There is a basic planning process in use throughout our society today, in the church as well as in other institutions, which consists primarily of setting goals and objectives, listing and choosing from alternative strategies for reaching the goals, performing the tasks, and evaluating the results. While this process may work well in task-oriented organizations, it is our experience that it does not work well in the church because the process assumes that there is an ideal to be reached and that it can be accomplished by marshalling forces to *do* something. It does not work for the church because the church's purpose is relational rather than functional—being rather than doing. Planning for the church, therefore, requires a process based upon its relational character.

In relation to the community, the church's task is receiving people into the communion, the fellowship. Its purpose is to be the arena where people can talk about their yearnings, their strivings, and their hopes; the opportunity for people to understand the forces affecting their lives and the lives of their neighbors. Church services and meetings allow people to get a perspective on the totality of their lives, including their day-to-day involvements in families, schools, work, civic activities, and other relationships. It is a setting in which people can work out the norms and values by which they will govern their lives and in which the fragmentation of their existence can be centered and ordered.

The church, therefore, must plan on two levels. First, it must plan the occasions when the faithful come together. It also must participate in those other occasions when community people, many of whom are not church members, come together. The community is the larger constituency of the church. Sometimes the church plans events for the people of the community who are not identified with the church but whom the church identifies as its people. Some activities are for church members, others are for both members and nonmembers; and still others may be targeted for nonmembers only. For example, the Sunday school class and the congregational dinner are most often planned for members. The youth drop-in center, the senior citizens' club and the special musical programs are often attended by both members and nonmembers. The mission for transients, the halfway house for alcoholics, and the center for run-away youth are generally for nonmembers—means of offering the care, compassion, and hope of the people of God to people who may not have experienced God in that way before.

The congregation, therefore, plans both the occasions

when it comes together as a Body, and occasions when it shares its being with people outside the Body. Ministry takes place not as the members do something to or for the nonmembers, but as the members share who they are—who Christ is—and thereby offer the possibility of the outsiders becoming part of the Body too.

The pastor of a new church in a developing suburban community recently told about the death of a small child in the community. A delivery man had not secured the brakes on his truck. It rolled down a hill and struck the playing child. The pastor said that this event had a traumatic effect on the community. "People in our young community do not often think of death. Death is something that happens to old people." The mother suffered a nervous breakdown and was hospitalized. The father was left to "pick up the pieces" and care for the other children. One day this pastor called on the father, stated that he did not want to intrude, but wanted to express the love and concern of his congregation. He was essentially apologizing for coming since the family did not participate in his church. The father's quick reply was, "Come on in here! I was just needing to talk to someone who is closer to God than I am." The father did not want the pastor or the church to *do* something; he merely needed one of God's people to *be* there.

A congregation's planning for sharing its life with the total community varies according to the community's scope and character. The special-purpose church plans on the basis of what is unique about its life. A constant threat to the special-purpose church is the possibility that it will lose its distinctive quality, which effectively takes away the church's reason for being. A church in a Southern city was formed five years ago as a liberal alternative to the conservative bent of the other congregations of the same denomination in the area. For several years it was the only church in the city with both white and black members. Today few black members remain in the church, and its character is not essentially different from a number of other churches in the area.

Downtown, metropolitan regional, and many small-town churches, because they serve more than one neighborhood and hence have heterogeneous communities, cannot afford the luxury of planning programs and ministries in only one way. To serve their total areas well, it may be necessary for them to have several worship services, church school sessions, or programs of whatever type, each of a different character and scheduled at a different time of the week for the convenience of the diverse constituency. Most neighborhood and open-country churches can serve their communities with fewer events and activities.

In addition to planning their ministry at two levels, churches must also plan for two time periods: this one and the next one. In order to maintain its rapport with the community, a congregation plans its ministry for the community as it now exists, and anticipates the next stage in the community's life cycle. Although the future may be uncertain, the church must constantly monitor present realities for future possibilities. The newly developing congregation plans for both the present growing community and the coming period of stability. If the church does not attain sufficient strength in its developing period, it may not survive when growth is no longer possible. The church in the stable community similarly lives in the relatively certain present, but also plans for the time when community patterns will begin to change and a new population may begin to enter the area. The process continues throughout the community's life cycle. Each church must constantly involve itself in both short- and long-range planning processes.

Planning in the community–church relationship occurs when church leaders are knowledgeable about trends and processes in the community. It is not enough, however, to know what is happening in the environment. The church also has the difficult assignment of relating community forces and characteristics to the internal realities of the church and to the church's primary task.

Current population trends in America reveal that the large number of children born in the post–World War II era are now themselves marrying and having children. This fact comes on the heels of a period of decreasing births and disenchantment with the church by many young adults. It is interesting for a church to know that for the next two decades there will be a large number of young married couples and small children in many communities. Information collected over several generations shows that many people who participate in the church enter initially as young children in the early elementary school years or as young adults during the early years of marriage or child rearing. Churches that recognize the unusual opportunity for attracting young families may render significant ministries to these segments of the population in the years to come.

But there is one more step in the planning process for the churches that will actually attract and serve the young families. The churches that reach these people successfully will listen as the young parents and children express their concerns about their lives and will structure their ministry appropriately to relate the expressed needs to God through congregations of caring people. Those churches that assume that the present church structure is adequate, that people who want to go to church will do so, and that offering a friendly handshake to those who do come is all that is necessary will lose a special opportunity for ministry.

We have discussed here only one major trend in contemporary American society and its relationship to the ministry of the church. There are many other trends. What are the dominant trends in your community currently and how do they relate to the possibility of ministry by your church? In one community, unemployment is presently a major concern. The reaction of some of the churches in the community is to fret that some people cannot pay their pledges to the church. One church, however, has revamped its budget in order to free funds to hire some unemployed community residents to work for the church during this period. Another church, concerned about the impact of unemployment on family life, has organized several groups to give special support to affected families. Another church has directed its efforts to attracting additional employers to the area. The difference in how churches respond depends upon whether they believe and act as though the church exists for people rather than people existing to maintain the church.

In normal times most churches attempt to plan for all of the people in their communities, trying to have a full range of opportunities for both church members and outsiders. The only problem is that normal times are elusive—the community is never normal, unless normal is defined as moving from one concern, crisis, or pervasive condition to another. Seen in this way, the church has two primary roles in relationship to the community. On the one hand, it offers stability in the midst of change; on the other hand, it moves with the community through each phase or each crisis. The churches that render effective ministry perform both of these roles as they maintain a process of planning that systematically correlates the needs of the people of the community with God's continuing action in Christ.

The Management of Programing

Programing is a natural outgrowth of planning. Plans issue in events and activities in which community residents participate to understand their life situations and the Christian gospel, to seek and find the God who can help them deal with the ultimate concerns of their lives, and to prepare them to appropriate the gospel in their lives.

The problem with the planning–programing process in some congregations is that programing is the end of planning. If "good" or "helpful" programs are implemented, it is assumed that the planning is a success and that the primary task of the church is being fulfilled. This is the same fallacy in the typical planning process we pointed to earlier, the error of the pastor who wrote asking for "models of successful urban parishes," or the layman at a recent workshop who said "tell us what other churches are doing to get new members."

First, such an approach is a preoccupation with doing rather than being. Second, it is focusing on the institution rather than people. Third, it is a failure to see that vital programing grows out of the nature of the community, the self-identity of the congregation, the vision of congregational leaders, and the church's understanding of its reason for being. Fourth, this concept of programing sees the program as an end in itself rather than a means to the end of receiving people from the community and relating them to God. Relating the people to the church, or to the program itself, is believed to be sufficient.

Periodically many churches attempt to evaluate their existing programs. The criteria used in this evaluation process are critical—they reveal whether the programs have become the purpose of the church's efforts or whether there is a purpose beyond the programs. Where the program is the purpose, the measures of success are the number of people who attend, the expressed level of satisfaction by participants, and how long the program endures. But when programs are judged on the basis of their contribution to the church's primary task, success is measured by the ability of the church to reach out to all the people in the community and accept them in their need, the quality of lives redeemed as a result of having been related to God through the program, and the changing characteristics of the social milieu where those lives are lived. It is immediately apparent that the latter criteria are much more difficult to measure. Perhaps that is the reason we commonly revert to using the former measures.

Managing a program is fairly simple if the task if to get or keep people active. We only need to be creative in thinking up new programs as old ones lose their allure, to allocate adequate recourses to support the program, to publicize the activity among people who do not have enough to do or who perhaps feel guilty that they are not more "deeply involved" in the church, and to recruit willing and able leaders to administer the program.

Managing a program is not a simple matter if the program is to be intimately tied to both the needs of the community and the church's primary task. At a minimum the following considerations must be present:

1. Making the church visible and available. Some churches are located on major thoroughfares, so everyone in the community knows of their existence and has some knowledge about them. Metropolitan regional churches, by definition, are visible to large areas; otherwise they could not attract members from large areas. Small-town and open-country churches are also generally visible. Other churches may not be visible in their communities and thus may have limited opportunities for ministry. Sometimes neighborhood churches are so hidden that few people even in the immediate area know that they exist. Downtown churches that serve entire metropolitan areas have increasingly lost visibility as working and shopping patterns have

changed and fewer people participate in activities in downtown areas.

The location of a congregation's building is only one way that it achieves visibility in the community. The church may become known by the quality of its programing, by advertisements in the media, by radio and television programs, or by word of mouth as participants talk to their neighbors. A church's ministry is limited by the number of people who know of its existence and have a positive image of its role in the community. The methods appropriate to gaining visibility and projecting a positive and open image depend upon both the nature and scope of the community and the church's creativity in using available resources.

2. Letting the people talk. Often people are able to get in touch with their deepest needs and yearnings as they are given the opportunity to verbalize them. Is it possible that some people who attend church regularly are always talked *to* and do not have the opportunity to talk about their own lives and what they want their lives to become? Is the program structure of your church such that people can talk freely about their faith, about what God is doing in their lives, and about what they want God to do for and with them in the future? What about the people in the community who are not related to a church? Are the members of the congregation trained and challenged to be good listeners—listening wherever they encounter people for dreams that may never have been heard before?

3. Sorting out target populations. Based on what it has heard from its community, a church must be able to differentiate categories of concerns and groups of people who have common needs and interests. Retail department stores, which are not unlike churches in that participation is voluntary and people may have several from which to choose, have long recognized that they must tailor the nature and quality of their goods, their displays, and their advertisements for specific audiences. A newspaper story about a major department store in a midwestern city related that recent research has indicated that the store has two major customers: "the budget-minded shopper living in the immediate area of the store, and the affluent shopper from surrounding communities." The store will soon

"create a separate budget store and expand and upgrade the sales area in the main store," the manager pointed out, because "it was difficult to come up with a plan to serve both under the same roof."[1]

Churches must also learn to understand the differences among people in their communities. Segmenting the population of the community is not to deny the church's ministry to any of them; rather, it is the only way to be sure that all people in the community are included.

4. Recruiting and training indigenous leaders. If you have ever been associated with a church in a posttransitional community, you know how rare it is for the leaders to live in the community. Almost universally, the pastor and the lay leaders live in a different community. The phenomenon is not limited to posttransitional communities; it is common in older neighborhood and open-country churches. The leadership of downtown churches today often resides in the suburbs. The result is that those parts of the community where the leaders live get most of the church's attention.

In communities changing racially or socially, older members often are reluctant to relinquish leadership to the newer residents of the area, sometimes believing that the new people do not know how to lead, or have not been in the church long enough to have earned the right. Churches that stay in touch with their communities will not let this happen.

5. Relating to other churches. Churches are often involved in program endeavors that can be strengthened by cooperative efforts with other churches. Where interchurch cooperation is feasible, it is to be encouraged. An important factor in the success of such ventures is the number of types of churches involved. If the program is citywide in scope, for example, churches participating generally should be downtown churches whose communities extend across the entire area; few neighborhood churches get excited about metropolitan issues. Cooperation among churches with different communities is generally successful only in issues

---

[1] *The Kettering-Oakwood Times* (Kettering, Ohio: Times Publications), October, 29, 1977, p. 29.

affecting all or part of the communities of each church.

6. Evaluating programs. We discussed earlier the necessity of measuring the success of programs in terms of their contribution to the church's primary task. To be helpful, evaluation of individual programs must also be related to progress toward the attainment of short- or long-term goals (depending on why the program was established), other programs designed to accomplish the same goals, and the availability of resources. Sometimes successful programs cost more than their contribution justifies. A great problem in many churches may be that the minister's time is taken up with running programs that look pleasing but accomplish little of the church's basic tasks.

Managing programing in the way we have discussed it here is never simple. The programing system requires constant overseeing by the pastor, large time contributions by lay leaders, and continued monitoring. It is primarily through programing, however, that people are related to God in the congregation and members are prepared for reaching out in ministry to others. It demands our best management efforts.

8

The Management of Ministry
Through Structure

Examining the life of a church and changing that life are
indivisible processes. Like putting one's hand into a bucket of
water to feel what is at the bottom, it is not possible to investigate without altering the situation.

Groups are the building blocks of church structure—formal groups designated by denominational charter or local by-
laws, and informal groups formed by the multiform web of
associational forces. For some groups maintaining emotional
investments will seem to be a central task. Many groups will
also have definite work tasks to be performed in the maintenance of church fabric and in the furtherance of its mission.

The management of the structure of ministry is essentially
a task of assisting the various groups to discover their own
situation and to lead them in the shaping of an exciting and
apostolic future vision. Free, informed, and committed choice is
the result of a continuous process of leadership, communication, and problem solving. The change process is a continuous,
unbroken movement of clarification and amplification of our
ability to act upon opportunities and to overcome the inevitable
problems and obstacles.

The Management of Task Groups

The nature of most of the tasks to be accomplished in a
church demand that a group of people be involved; few tasks
are genuinely the work of a single individual. Most parish leaders would hope that these groups would be highly motivated;

that they could be settings for authentic Christian community; that they would do high-quality work; that they would collaborate with other committees, task forces, and groups in the congregation; and that they would be characterized by a high degree of initiative and self-direction. Because of the value of a shared ministry based upon a broad distribution of control and because they are unable to be present at every group meeting, clergy generally wish for, but often despair of finding, energetic, self-directed working committees and groups. The ability to create and maintain such groups is important to the management of ministry. Many clergy have been trained in group process skills, but they tend to see them as the only remedy for poorly functioning work groups.

This section deals with what is a more complex but a more practical approach to the management of church work groups.

The Start-up of a Task Group

The most important period in the life of a group is its moment of birth. Three elements of a church group organized for work that are crucial to effective performance are: (1) the nature of the *task;* (2) the *composition* of the group; and (3) the work *procedure.* All three of these areas are influenced most easily as the group is brought into being. Leadership effort spent on the careful design and start-up of a group will have payoff for months to come.

We recommend starting any important new church group with an overnight conference. The conference should be a time for fun, prayer, and the hard work of clarifying the group task and adopting sound procedures for accomplishing the work. Roles must be defined and people helped to feel comfortable in them.

The composition of a group, particularly a volunteer group, is almost impossible to change once the group is operating. Unfortunately, the only question about group composition that most church leaders seem to consider important is: "Is the group representative of the congregation?" This may be the least relevant criterion that should be applied. We suggest two criteria for determining group composition: (1) Does the group possess sufficient skill and knowledge as related to the task? (heterogeneity); and (2) Is there sufficient common ground for the group to coalesce? (homogeneity). The application of these different criteria to essentially the same task can be illustrated by two recent examples. In both instances the minister wished to create a group to provide evaluation and feedback.

The first pastor selected a group of three men and three women, all of whom were notable for their interpersonal skill, their capacity for thoughtful reflection, and their basically forthright approach to church life. The group ranged in age from thirty-five to sixty. Four of the six had held positions of responsible leadership within the church. Meeting once a month over a period of nine months, this group succeeded in providing the minister with a sense of their support and concern for him as a person and as a man of God. They also were able to confront the minister candidly and sensitively with aspects of his leadership that had become severely damaging to the life of the church.

The second pastor convened a gathering of ten women and eight men, ranging in age from twenty-one to sixty-two. The minister stated that his criterion for selection was broad representation of the congregation and that he had included some specific individuals in the group because he hoped they would learn and grow from the situation. Three members of the group were quite new members of the church; eight were experienced leaders in the church. The remaining seven people represented a scattered, typical range of church experience.

The group met only a few times and never accomplished its task, and it ended simply by not being reconvened. The group was so large that it could not carry on the kind of free-flowing discussion that was needed. Several individuals in the group were unable to listen attentively and to accept the contributions of the other group members. The range of values and perception present in the group made the task of simple communication overwhelmingly difficult when the group touched on sensitive areas.

The specified task of personal evaluation did demand honest feedback that represented all segments of the congregation.

The design of the first group allowed this to happen in a way that averted a major congregational battle because the group size and composition allowed it to reach the level of insight and trust necessary to free the enormously sensitive issues involved. The group possessed the interpersonal skill and the theological acumen necessary for the job. They had proven skill in representing the congregation. The group was small enough and homogeneous enough so that the members were able to draw together behind a solid investment in one another and in the job to be done. As the failure of the second group dramatically demonstrates, there is a sharp difference between a group with skills necessary to represent the congregation and a group simply based on representation.

Once a group has been formed and structured, it can be very difficult to change. By attending carefully to the initial makeup of the group—looking for compatibility and the necessary skills—and by helping the group to a good start, much later confusion and difficulty can be avoided.

The work of a church task group

The most subtly enervating factor for volunteers is the absence of the proper kind of work. To get paid to do work that doesn't seem personally significant is one thing; to voluntarily associate in a common mission repeatedly expressed in tasks that seem insignificant or never come to fruition is quite another matter. Volunteer work, and certainly the work of the church, can be structured to be significant and to make an effective contribution to society.

The best way to check up on the nature of the work is to ask the people engaged in its performance. Basing our conclusions on the research of Richard Hackman of Yale University,[1] we have found that the answers to three general questions will provide a great deal of insight into the experienced meaningfulness of work.

---

[1] J. Richard Hackman, "The Design of Self Managing Work Groups," *Technical Report No. 11* (New Haven, Conn.: School of Organization and Management, Yale University, December 1976).

1.   To what degree does the task draw upon valued skills? (Volunteer work is an ideal situation for the use of skills that are very valuable but are underutilized or relatively untested in normal work and career.)

2.   Is the task identifiable? Is it a whole piece of work with a visible outcome?

3.   To what degree will this work have impact upon the lives of others?

The sum of these three criteria is a good indication of the meaning of the work itself. Standing committees are particularly prone to low ratings on these questions—their work too often seems to become the performance of procedural roles rather than the completion of significant tasks. Thus the Christian education committee assumes the procedural role of somehow being responsible for the whole of Christian education. The task identity has become so diffuse that the potential significant impact of their work is never realized, and people feel frustrated in the exercise of their skills.

As work progresses, two more questions become important in determining the motivation of the group:

1.   To what degree does the group feel responsible for the outcome of its work?

2.   To what degree is the group receiving knowledge of the results of its work?

Much of the work of the local church is not concrete and quantifiable. Even when we can count heads or dollars, so many factors influence what happens that it is difficult to assign responsibility or measure results. But this fact does not account for the vast majority of the deficient answers to these questions.

An important aspect to consider in using these two questions is the degree of interdependence the task requires. An athletic team such as a soccer team can be held responsible because of the tremendous degree of interdependence required by its work. In contrast, a committee whose major group work is to hear reports of individual task assignments has a much more limited and less visible interdependence. In this instance only the chairperson is accountable for the group as a whole. Many church groups are more like a swim team than a soccer team. Each person is churning away in his or her lane, but there is no actual interdependence around the work to be done. In other words, these questions can uncover the fact that the group tasks are not group work at all but rather the sum of a number of individual tasks.

Either way of working can be appropriate and effective. The issue is to remain clear as to whether one is dealing with a group task or an individual task. A great frustration of committee work stems from the sense the work would be done faster and better without the burden of the other members. If a task really belongs to an individual give it to the person so that he can feel responsible and can receive knowledge of the results of his work. A good group task is a task that, like winning a soccer game, can only be accomplished through group effort.

Working by the rules

The ways a group sets about doing its work is an important determinant of its effectiveness. Church boards typically use the same work methods for the most complex ministry tasks as they do for routine chores. Indeed, Hackman's research indicates that the members of a work group "typically share a set of expectations about the 'proper' way to carry out the work, routinely behave in accord with those expectations, and enforce to some degree adherence to them." Thus groups have norms of the acceptable way to do work and leave little room for testing the appropriateness of their strategies.

Unnoticed and reinforced bad work habits abound in church groups. A large clergy staff never uses an agenda. No one chairs the meeting. The discussions are punctuated by entertaining but diverting stories that come to the minds of various staff members. By simply changing one work habit, a church board is transformed. Ineffectual lethargy is replaced by a growing sense of excitement over the group's increasing movement. In one instance this transformation occurred because the board adopted a new work norm they called an action list. In the past board decisions had simply been noted in the minutes;

the action list agreement forced the group to go a step further. Every decision now required three implementing decisions, which were listed on a single sheet of paper with three columns like those below:

What	Who	By when
Appoint an Executive Committee	Jane Green	October 15

The action list forced the group to specify the major tasks to be done, who was going to be responsible, and the date by which the task was to be completed. The list revealed the fact that many past decisions had been little more than momentary agreements about hoped-for future action, and that the specific decisions needed to turn hope into reality had never been completed. Among the most common, inadequate work group procedures are the following:

Over-reliance on Robert's Rules of Order.   Roberts' Rules are an important regulatory device for political and parliamentary bodies. They provide a widely accepted means of ordering debate and facilitating voting by contesting political camps. It is an extremely inadequate and cumbersome procedure for a group engaged in complex problem-solving procedures, but unfortunately, Robert's Rules are the only device many church groups possess to structure their work.

Habitual use of a discussion-group approach to problem solving.   When groups turn away from Robert's Rules because it is an inappropriate structure for their task, they often lapse into the habits of a bull session or discussion group. Common results of this approach include lost time, compounded ignorance, failure to consider more than one alternative, and unclear decision making.

At the least, interdependent task groups need to learn and become proficient at structures for problem solving such as the one outlined in Chapter 9. When an issue of ministry development arises the leader must be able to structure the work in a clear and consistent fashion. Just because you are departing from parliamentary procedure doesn't mean that you need no structure at all to guide the group in its deliberations. Use a chart pad or blackboard. Help the group decide if it is ready to solve the problem or capitalize on the opportunity being discussed. At each decision point check the consensus with the group. Once the decision has been made ask the group to identify all information pertinent to the concern. List the main points for all to see. Check to be certain that the information is complete. Now the information can be sifted and analyzed to surface critical relationships and priority issues. Once again the differing perspectives of group members can significantly enhance the quality of the work. Group consensus should emerge around the most important and workable directions to be taken. Identify these items on the board and check the consensus with the group. Now the group can be asked for its ideas about how to go the direction it has decided. Hold the floor open for several alternatives to be presented and discussed. The work is not over when a choice has been made. Now the group must flesh out the decision and assign responsibility for its implementation. Such a procedure needs to be as accepted for task groups as Robert's Rules are for a legislative body.

Diverse tasks require different work strategies and procedures. Many professional fund raisers recommend a work strategy that involves the chairperson of the fund campaign recruiting two assistant directors. The chairperson is asked to select people he or she knows well and can influence, and who would do a good job. In a similar fashion each assistant campaign director recruits two or three helpers, using the same criteria, and so on down the line. No one is ever asked to work with more than four or five people, and no one is asked to work with a stranger. This strategy works remarkably well. It generates clear task identity and responsibility. It can be easily adopted by smaller groups as a means of parceling out work.

Inadequate reports and records.   Volunteer groups, in particular, need clear, accurate records and reports. One of the unique characteristics of volunteer groups is that volunteers lack the advantage of close, daily contact with their fellow workers. Days and weeks go by without interaction between members to remind them of the tasks and issues at hand; workers in the church often have to content themselves with a monthly meeting and an occasional phone call. Continuity of work becomes more dependent than ever upon easily obtained and clearly understood reports and records. The action list has already been cited; Three other procedures have proven quite useful.[2]

1.   A three-part agenda format, as illustrated below:

Item	Background	Action Needed
Steeple repair	Bad leaks. Bids have been solicited from three roofers.	Decision on the recommendation of the Maintenance Committee.

This agenda form helps remind people why items are being considered, forces the leadership to clarify and order the business, and specifies the action the group needs to take. Some groups add a fourth column which is headed "action taken" so that members may keep a record on the agenda form of the group decisions. An agenda such as this can also indicate the priority weight of agenda items by stating approximate time allocations for each item. An agenda as structured as this can still leave room for last minute additions by any group member. What it does require is some thought by the member regarding the nature of the item and the reasons for placing it on the agenda.

2.   The adoption of a "bucket" list. A "bucket" list is simply a formal procedure for recording issues of concern that arise during work on other agenda items. These are separate but related problems or issues that need to be addressed. Without such a list these items either become diversions from the immediate work or are lost and forgotten until necessity forces the concern at some later time.

---

[2]We are grateful for the suggestions of Dale Lake's unpublished paper, "Improving Group Decision Making," for many of these work-group concepts.

3.   Working notebooks. The habit of maintaining a notebook for each group member is useful as a means of
providing historical continuity. Such notebooks can contain the group's minutes, a log of key decisions, role
assignments and descriptions. For standing committees
with high turnover, the procedure is a valuable means of
orienting new members. At least one complete notebook
should be kept in the church office for each working
committee.

Either good or bad work habits can seem relatively insignificant elements of church structure. Like most habits they are
unconsciously perpetuated; it is easy for those with the habit
to brush off critical comment on its ill effects. Therefore, it often
takes the help of an outsider for a group to change its work
habits. Work-group practices are a critical area of local church
structure, and they deserve careful consideration.

The Analysis and Support of the Family of the Church

The idea that groups are important to human beings seems
so well accepted as to be scarcely worth special notice. Who
would want to be without friends and some form of belonging.
From the moment of our birth into the primal organization of
the family, we spend the major share of our lives in social
settings. Most of us readily assume that an important determinant of our behavior is the nature of our interactions within
significant groups. The dominance of organizations in our lives
requires, however, that we step back to view with more dis-
crimination the nature of church belonging as contrasted with
other forms of organizational membership. If the groups we
belong to are important determinants of our growth, are some
more important than others? Because we use similar labels for
various groups, it is easy to assume that a fellowship group is
a fellowship group is a fellowship group, and to overlook the
extreme differences in patterns of interaction that occur in
groups and social settings that share a common designation.
Some soils are barren, lacking the nutrients to support rich
growth. How important is the garden of life together for

spiritual development, and what nutrients and climate are needed for such growth to occur?

The issue at stake is vital. Over the last decade we have been able to visit and know firsthand a large number and range of congregations. We have worked with pastors, congregational leaders, and teams of consultants, and the impact of our personal experience has convinced us that church groups do have a powerful influence on the well-being of their members and that this influence is often more negative than positive. For example, one consultant has said about her experience with the search committee of a congregation seeking a new pastor: "I can't stand the way they treat one another in that committee. Putdowns are the rule of the day. Hardly anyone really gets listened to, and I think most decisions are really made over the telephone before the meeting ever begins."

This congregation has a large and loyal membership. Is the consultant's experience simply the result of her own perception? Can we assume that a large and flourishing membership is a sign of healthy communal life? Different people are looking for different things, but is that sufficient explanation for the consultant's observations? More important, what we are searching for in this instance is the fundamental proposition of sickness and health. When the consultant says, "I can't stand the way they treat one another in that committee," is it not possible that what she is saying goes far beyond questions of personal style to the fact she literally can't stand that form of life together because it is unhealthy?

There is certainly abundant evidence that groups have power to heal or to cripple. From New Testament times to the present, the church has been witness to the realization of the healing of that unity of body and soul we call spirit:

Is any among you sick? Let him call for the elders of the church, and let them pray over him, annointing him with oil in the name of the Lord (James 5:14, RSV).

Numerous studies are beginning to clarify the relationship between health and the presence and strength of interpersonal social supports. Studies in World War II showed that the interpersonal support present in a bomber crew helped sustain the members under the stress of battle. A recent study demonstrated that pregnant women undergoing a great deal of stress or change had a high rate of complications during pregnancy. However, the study went further to show that the women under high stress but with highly supportive social systems had no more complications than women with histories of low stress.[3] There is also evidence that the nature of the family's interpersonal environment is a major determinant of juvenile delinquency problems and of the potential outcome of treatment.[4]

As we now commonly assume that family and peer group are powerful forces shaping the development of children and youth, so today we are becoming aware of the importance of primary group belonging for the passages of adult life. Rites of passage do not stop at puberty, and both critical life events and the normal life course elicit new developmental journeys. No life is free of the need for supportive community. As one parish pastor describing the difficulty of developing lay leadership suddenly exclaimed, "Well, for one thing, almost everyone I've got in a position of leadership is going through some kind of personal crisis. They can't take leadership because it is all they can do to contend with their own lives." I responded to his comment by describing the possibility I had seen realized in some church groups—groups that not only accomplish their tasks but become for the members a primary source of healing and support during a critical life passage. The pastor replied, "Is that really possible?"

Believing and working toward the fulfillment of this possibility is the essence of Christian community.

Virginia Satir, a contemporary pioneer in the field of family counseling, has worked with thousands of family groups. We believe that the idea of family is a useful means of defining Christian community, and we see Satir's model for the "peoplemaking" qualities of a family as extremely

---

[3]John Cassel, "Psychosocial Processes and Stress—Theoretical Formulation," *International Journal of Health Services,* vol. 4, No. 3, 1974.
[4]Rudolf H. Moos and Bernice S. Moos, "A Typology of Family Social Environments," *Family Process,* vol. 15, no. 4, December 1976.

useful.[5] She says that there are four aspects of family life that crop up time and again with the troubled families who come to her for help. In her opinion, these four forces or factors determine whether or not the family is making itself healthy and whole or sick and troubled. The four elements of family life are self-worth, communication, rules, and linking to society. Satir has contrasted her experience with troubled families and nurturing families in the following manner:

Troubled Family	Nurturing Family
Self-worth is low.	Self-worth is high.
Communication is indirect, vague, not really honest.	Communication is direct, clear, specific, and honest.
Rules are rigid, inhuman, nonnegotiable, and everlasting.	Rules are flexible, human, appropriate, and subject to change.
Linking to society is fearful, placating, and blaming.	Linking to society is open and hopeful.

It is Satir's experience that families can learn how to be more nurturing, and that almost all families must work to improve their peoplemaking qualities—it doesn't come easily or naturally: "Alas, only four families in perhaps a hundred know how to do it."

We believe that the family of God can change to become more nurturing but that it doesn't happen for most groups without conscious attention and work. At the *least*, it seems to us, church fellowship groups (sentient or reference groups) should be working toward the qualities of a nurturing family. After some years of involvement in human relations training, we got used to some church folk complaining that "the group dynamics people" never talk about God in their groups. The complaint has some validity to it, but it ignores the priority of rectifying the sick and distorted practices of life found in too many Christian communities. For church people to put something down as "mere humanism" is narrow and self defeating. The distinctive religious nature of group life in the church does not exclude consideration of the need for groups to work to-

---

[5]Virginia Satir, *Peoplemaking* (Palo Alto, Calif.: Science and Behavior Books, 1972).

ward becoming more humane and nurturing in their enduring interpersonal interactions. As Hans Kung reminds us, "God's cause is not cult but man. Service of God never excuses from service to man: it is in service to man that service to God is proved."[6]

Satir's categories give us an important, clear, and easily applicable means of ministry with the human supports of congregational group structure.

As an individual invests loyalty and sentiment in a church group, the group becomes a standard of reference for values, ideals, and perceptions of self. The expectations of the group become powerful influences upon the behavior and roles the person chooses. Every such group will have accustomed, patterned ways of relating to other groups in the congregation and the community. It will have its rules, written or unwritten, about what is acceptable or not acceptable. It will have a style or pattern of communication. And, inevitably, the group will enhance or erode the self-esteem of its members. In other words, such a group is a school for learning how to relate to those who are different, for learning reinforced patterns of communication, for the inculcation of rules and values for living, and for gaining an important image of who we are as individuals.

For example, take Carol, who has worked long and hard for her congregation. During the last eight years she and her friend Sue have been largely responsible for revamping the Sunday morning Christian education program. Her primary affiliations during the eight years were in the church council and a small education committee composed of herself, Sue, and two other lay people. Carol recalls with the humor of hindsight the suspicion the education committee had of the church council in the early years of her effort. The decision by the committee to be direct, open, and confronting of the council for their lack of support for Christian education stands out in her mind as a time of major importance in her life. She says that only the support of the group made it possible for her to really take such a stand.

---

[6]Hans Kung, *On Being A Christian* (Garden City, N. Y.: Doubleday, 1976).

Eventually Carol was elected to the church council. She cherishes the memory of the council's annual overnight conference, the hard fights and the good times. She says it was here that she really learned that she could stand up and speak out for her beliefs and values.

A couple of years ago Carol moved into a new stage of her life. She began to think seriously about work and a career. She began to question her relationship with her husband—a relationship in which she now began to see a lot of childish behavior on her part and reinforcement for this role from her husband. Carol began spending much less time as a volunteer worker at the church. But she has now begun to feel that she broke a rule somewhere along the line, for she has noticed a real change in the quantity and quality of interaction she now has with her circle of church friends. She gets the impression from some remarks, though no one has directly confronted her, that several people feel she has gotten carried away with "the women's lib bit." The curve of Carol's self-esteem has had sharp up and down movements in recent months as she attemps to cope and make sense of her new life passage.

Carol's story shows the way individual values become group norms and norms influence individual behavior, attitudes, and emotions. To speak of a group's unspoken rules is just another way of describing its norms. Church members, like Carol's friend, Sue, had been affectionate, considerate, and loyal to Carol. In part, because of them, the church had become a primary reference group for Carol, shaping her values and perception of life. She had internalized her friends' values of how a "good Christian woman" behaves. She had striven, almost without realizing it, to achieve that value. Now with new friends and relationships entering her life she was beginning to experience a conflict between freshly won perceptions of a good woman and her old church ties.

It is important to note that at one level Carol's conflict was inevitable. People do hold different values. Individual values do get transplanted into unspoken rules and definitions regarding "a good member" of the group. When someone breaks a rule that person inevitably experiences some form of rejection or disapproval. As soon as Carol began to invest herself in a new group with values different from her past associations, her internal conflict was indeed inevitable. The relevant learning in Carol's story is that the depth issues and emotions of her experience went unnoticed and unexamined by the people most important to her. Her church friends were still her friends. They wanted to be sympathetic and supportive to her. The thought that they were actually being insensitive or unfriendly would have been devastating to them. They discussed means of remaining in contact with Carol. They would have been hurt and surprised to be called disloyal to her.

Unfortunately this discussion and problem solving took place at a level which excluded the possibility of the human encounter that was needed. Missing from the conversation was an expression of the frustration and disappointment that was felt on both sides. Absent from the problem solving was any opening to fundamentally redefine the problem. The group had expressed the issue in its own terms: how can we stay friends with Carol and keep her involved in church activities. A different definition would have been: how can we talk about what we mean to each other and do to one another? That this conversation never took place is a witness not to any lack of love or concern but to the habits of life together in Carol's congregation. The church members often talked about programs and activities to make people feel welcome. It would have seemed strange and embarrassing to talk at the level of direct, specific, honest reaction to one another. Carol didn't need the agreement of her church friends. She certainly wasn't hoping that they could scheme ways to remain in friendly contact with her. Her most important need was to be treated seriously, to hear the direct and candid reaction of her friends, to be confronted as an adult making free choices rather than sympathetically tolerated like a middle-age adolescent seeking her identity. But Carol and her church friends had never learned how to talk about the people-making qualities of their life together.

Many groups, and indeed most churches, have what Steele

and Jenks call supernorms.[7] These are norms that inhibit the examination of group habits. Unspoken rules that say:

1.   We don't talk about embarrassing issues.

2.   We deal with problems in a cool, rational manner. Emotions will get in the way.

3.   We remember that being friendly means being polite at all times.

These are rules that impede a group's learning about its own climate of emotional support and interpersonal health. In our experience the most common and most grievously damaging behavior in church groups is the existence of these supernorms, particularly in the relationship between clergy and laity. In the name of love and friendship the group never tells the pastor that he often runs evening meetings in a rambling, incoherent fashion. Gossip and speculation move through the congregation from time to time about the pastor's possible alcoholic tendencies. Programs are invented in the hopes they will compensate for his lack of accountable follow-through in church affairs. Consultants are hired to remotivate the dispirited leadership. Rump groups meet to share their bitterness at the ways they have been treated. As situations like this persist for years and years, the supernorms grow stronger; "how could we possibly talk about something this embarrassing and damaging". The pastor's perceptions of self and situation grow more and more distorted. The pastor's feeling of self worth sinks lower and lower. He is unable to share the bitterness and disappointment he feels. When leaders meet to discuss congregational goals and problems, there is always present a powerful, unspoken, censoring set of rules screening out a whole level of information fundamental to the issues at hand. Often we have seen this cycle end in personal and institutional disaster. Only when the situation has progressed far beyond what is embarrassing and painful to the realm of individual disgrace, to open warfare in the congregation between those "for the pastor" and those

---

[7]Fritz Steele and Stephen Jenks *The Feel of the Work Place.* (Reading: Addison-Wesley, 1977).

"against," and to actions to remove the minister does the truth finally surface.

Unwritten rules such as these are a part of a circular self-reinforcing process. Leadership shapes the rules, and the leaders are influenced by the rules. Leaders are chosen who fit the rules, and one becomes a leader by conforming to the rules. Because the rules apply to the relationship with the key leader, the minister, they come to apply to all church member relations.

In the same fashion, however, it is the leadership that has the power to break the rules and to change the rules. Only the minister can say, "I know that many of you are disappointed in my leadership. I want to look at what is going wrong, and, if the problem is that I am the wrong person for this marriage, I'll leave." Only key leaders can say to other members, "I'm tired of hearing private complaints about the pastor. It's time you spoke your feelings in public. I'm willing to lead if we can get these issues in the open." It is from actions such as these that the climate is built which could have led to a happier ending to Carol's story.

There are several things any group can and ought to do to consciously address the forces of individual–group interaction, so strongly evident in Carol's story. All of them, however, add up to one essential: the willingness to stop and take the time to talk candidly about the here-and-now relationships among the members of the group:

> Does it feel good to be a part of this group?
>
> Do you feel you are with people you can trust and who trust you?
>
> Do you usually leave the group with your spirit high or low?
>
> What is said and done when a mistake is made or a difference arises?

As Satir writes, "Feelings of worth can only flourish in an atmosphere where individual differences are appreciated, mistakes are tolerated, communication is open, and the rules are flexible—the kind of atmosphere that is found in a nurturing family."

The following suggestions can be guides for groups attempting to create such communication:

1. Use Satir's four categories:
    Self-worth
    Communication
    Rules
    Linking to others
    as the outline to structure your group review. The clearer the structure for your review, the more people will be able to enter into such discussion.

2. It is often easiest at the beginning to have each person write his or her answer to a question and post the answers anonymously. This allows people a little more security for such self-revelation and also gives everyone an immediate sense of the range of perceptions and feelings in the group.

3. Such discussions are enhanced by initial ground rules, for instance:
    Feelings are facts—not to be debated or denied.
    Feelings need to be owned—notice the difference in saying, "You make me mad," or "The lonely little boy in me gets angry when you don't build on my contribution to the group discussion."
    Identify specific behavior, specific incidents, not just general perceptions—notice the difference in saying, "I really like being a part of this group," or "Sam and Ruth, I really felt good about the care you took in asking about my new situation at work."

4. In particular, remember that it may take an outside group or person to both jolt you and assist you into the awareness of your community life. In clinical training I encountered a young woman who had grown up in an isolated rural family in which her mother and father had taught her that incest was perfectly right and proper. Groups, like families, create their own isolated culture, which can and do become distorted bearers of values and life practice. The more closed the group, the more likely this is to

happen. Opening the door to an outside resource person can be essential for growth.

Whether a group is temporary or permanent; whether we call it a study group, a cell, or a friendship group; or whether it even has formal status, we believe that the face-to-face, nurturing, sustaining, loving primary group belongings are the bricks and mortar of the American congregation. The larger the church, the more heterogeneous the mission neighborhoods, the more difficult it is to create such settings and maintain them as a part of the whole. But despite the challenge, it is in such settings that the basic trust is developed that is the prerequisite for faith development.

9

Leadership and the Management of Ministry

Psychological Contract and Covenant—Dual Leadership Responsibilities

Bring together in one room the members of a local church and ask them to talk about their congregational experience. Get them to talk as individuals—"Talk for yourself and not for others." They should speak about what is uniquely rewarding or dissatisfying to them as individuals. Don't mix all of the comments together to try to find common themes or majority voices. This is like pouring several random cans of different color paint into one large pot—the distinctive colorations are lost, and the resultant blend is probably just a mess. Instead, like a child's dot-to-dot drawing, move from one person to the next, allowing each individual to take his or her unique position within the congregation. The more dots, the more exactly placed, the clearer will be the eventual picture of the church. Some people will be different from the majority, and their places in the congregation may indeed be far removed from the other clusters. Listen carefully as people talk, and it soon becomes apparent that several different types and levels of information are being presented.

Much of what people say is indistinguishable from comments that would be made by the members of any organization:

"The floors are dusty."

"I enjoy the meals."

"I like the people I work with."

"I've asked for a key three times and still haven't received it."

"The work of our committee has been aimless."

This level of information describes people's experience of the church as an institution or bureaucracy. They might make similar comments about the company for which they work, their local bank, or the neighboring supermarket.

A second level of comment stems from the experience of the church as a voluntary association. The mutuality of the Body is expressed in statements such as:

"When we were ill, several families brought food."

"I look to the church as a place where I can join with others in community service."

"The opportunities here have allowed me to learn about leadership skills I didn't know I had."

"In point of fact, the committee chairman never followed through on his assignments."

Such comments are similar to what might be said by the members of a civic association or volunteer service organization. They stem from the voluntary service aspect of the church's life.

The third level of commentary is related to the specific Christian character of the church. The issues are the degree to which the local church embodies the expected characteristics of a Christian congregation. Comments will touch on the quality of the preaching, the warmth or coldness of the fellowship, the availability and nature of the pastoral services, and the mood of worship.

A fourth, final level of comment will relate to the most private and personal dimension of an individual's church experience. This is the mediational role of the church in the shaping of an individual's relationship with the Divine:

"I'm really in despair over what has happened to me."

"My experience in the prayer and meditation group has changed my whole way of seeing things."

"I enjoy being active in the church, but I don't really think I'm a Christian."

Comment in this area will touch not only experience in the church but the whole of peoples' life space.

Assessing the climate of a congregation involves allowing individual expression and discriminating among the levels of each person's comment. The first two levels involve the leadership in the maintenance of a valid psychological contract. The second two levels present leadership with the responsibility of maintaining an authentic covenant relationship. The levels of information and their relationship can be diagramed as in Figure 6. An in-depth examination of the life of a church will contain comprehensive information for all four areas of experience. If the information is extensive and candid, part of what will be revealed is the spread or concentration of the experience among these four domains. Something of the style of a church is found in the relative emphasis on bureaucratic institution on the one hand and contemplative path to God on the other.

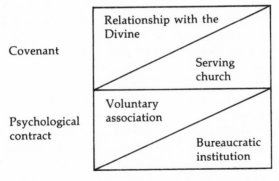

Figure 6. The Levels and Relationship of Information.

A psychological contract forms between every individual and the organization. Although such membership contracts go unwritten and almost always unstated, they constitute the reciprocal obligation between the member and the church. Like any contract, the psychological contract can be faithfully fulfilled, dishonored by default, or invalidated by the actions of either party. An attainable task of leadership is the fulfillment of conditions for the creation and support of a valid psychological contract between the individual and the organization. The psychological contract in the church is twofold—one aspect is the contract between institution and institutional member, which may feel similar to the relationship between doctor and patient or between employer and employee; the second aspect is the unspoken agreement between the association and its volunteer member, which may feel similar to the mutual obligations between union and union member or between political party and party worker. For individuals who experience the church as a Body of which all baptized people are members, this side of the psychological contract will probably be far more prominent than the institutional.

The main point is that leaders need to be sensitive to the wide range and varied nature of the expectations people have of the church. The leaders live in the tension of creating an equally flexible response to a wide range of member needs that is balanced by the critical continuity of scriptural and apostolic tradition. Recall that the Presbyterian membership study noted that one characteristic of growing congregations was a formal membership class for new members; this is probably in part because of the firmness and clarity of the psychological contract that can be built during the course of such a class.

We have chosen the word *covenant* to indicate the area of mutual obligation that is beyond the brick and mortar of general organizational experience. *Contract* implies a relationship freely entered into by both partners, a relationship marked by specific content, mutual obligations, and defined boundaries. The biblical concept of covenant retains these aspects of contract but with a crucial qualification: "God's voluntary initiation of the covenant relationship in history constantly serves to remind men that the character of the Sinai covenant is utterly different from that of human contracts, for as a gift of God's grace it lays stress on his rights to dispose all things as he wills."[1] Contract brings to mind union negotiations, legal ma-

---

[1]Walter Eichrodt, *Theology of the Old Testament* (Philadelphia: Westminster, 1961).

neuvers, and letter-of-the-law compliance. Covenant should suggest forbearance, grace, truth, and the claim of faith rather than legal code. It is fashionable these days to speak of marriage contracts. We still prefer the wording of the Book of Common Prayer, which talks of the bond and covenant of marriage: "It signifies to us the mystery of the union between Christ and his Church, and Holy Scripture commands it to be honored among all people."[2] Nevertheless, as the marriage contract movement has realized, covenant does not stand for an unexamined relationship of simple obedience. A covenant is like a contract in specifying a relationship of reciprocal and definable expectations.

The covenant aspects of the contract between member and church involve both the public ministries of the church and the private sojourn of the soul. The covenant quality of leader–member relationship implies that the nature of membership goes beyond involvement, loyal support, and organizational brick and mortar to the life of faith.

The reason we stress the issue of psychological contract and covenant is that the single most important variable in leadership effectiveness is the question of leader-member relationships. Whether one is managing a complicated task, or seeking to rally a group behind an important cause, or preaching a sermon, the thing which will have the single greatest impact on the effectiveness of the leadership offered is the quality of relationship between yourself and those you are trying to lead. Common sense says, and research verifies, that a leader who is well liked and respected does not need coercive power to influence subordinates and peers. The quality of the leader-member relationship is affected both by the loyalty and support the group gives the leader and by the quality of interpersonal relations among group members.[3] The more exactly and clearly you understand what members expect to give and receive, the more accurately you can work to provide clear information and to

---

[2] *The Book of Common Prayer—Proposed. According to the Use of the Episcopal Church* (New York: Seabury, 1977).
[3] Fred E. Fiedler *A Theory of Leadership Effectiveness.* (New York: McGraw Hill, 1967).

build sound contracts and covenants. Many times church leaders try to look for a task so exciting that people will just naturally be motivated and excited about its accomplishment. Much more important is time spent on strengthening the bonds between members and between leaders and members.

Some things every leader can do are:

1.   Recontract with group members;

2.   Devote more time, or less time, with those members who find the relationship with you particularly important. You are using your time with them as a positive or negative reinforcement of behavior;

3.   Spend more time being a conduit of information. The more people look to you to find out what is goign on, the more you will gain influence;

4.   Work to increase harmony within the group;

5.   Vary your availability to the group, the times you can be reached, and your openness to hear complaints.

Church leaders should also focus on the times and occasions when individuals call into question their contracts or covenants with the church. If a church member changes his or her job, it is a mistake to assume that the existing set of relationships, obligations, and expectations between that person and the church will continue unchanged. A baptism class for parents and god-parents is not just a time to transmit some information regarding the Christian heritage. It is an important moment to recontract new, mutual relationships and roles, obligations, and expectations between parents and church, as a result of the altered family situation. Any significant life change is an opportunity to revalidate the bond between member and congregation. From strong bonds come the power of effective leadership.

Learning is an organic process involving the whole person in community. There is an indissoluble link between Christian self-awareness, the appropriation of the Christian tradition, and the experienced norms and ideals of the community of faith. As Bernard Lonergan, S.J., states: "My unawareness is unexpressed. I have no language to express what I am, so I use the language of the tradition I unauthentically appropriate, and thereby I devaluate, distort, water down, corrupt that language. . . . So the unauthenticity of individuals becomes the unauthenticity of a tradition. Then in the measure a subject takes the tradition, as it exists, for his standard, in that measure he can do no more than authentically realize unauthenticity."[4]

In this cycle of interaction between the self and the congregation rests a major clue for the task of leadership. The responsibility of Christian leaders is to maintain a community that is an authentic bearer of the Christian covenant. Authentic appropriation, authentic community, and the responsible self-consciousness that leads to what Lonergan calls self-transcendence constitute a circular process of intellectual and social interactions. Spiritual direction must be as concerned with what is learned from the processes of socialization into institutional life as it is with individual programs of study, meditation, and counsel. Experienced perhaps only as a vague longing for salvation, hope is answered by the set of activities we encounter in the local church. In worship, in prayer, by sermons, in classes and activities, by the roles and relationships formed with pastor and people, this vague longing is given shape, form, and articulation.

Thus whatever may be the nature of a leader's theological answers, he or she encounters in each new setting a preexistent pattern of theological beliefs and attitudes embedded in a climate of structure and practice. However potent the theological seeds brought to the fields, there is already an existing ecology whose balance must be recognized and managed. To ignore these realities is to move blindly into the morass of a schizophrenic church—a church in which words, thoughts, and ideas have no relationship with the actual experience of people; an institution living with fantasy and delusions, while the actual life of its members, in committees, in interpersonal relationships, in the conduct of education and worship is solely an expression of the culture with only the vocabulary of illusion

---

[4]Bernard J. F. Lonergan, S.J., *Method in Theology* (New York: Herder and Herder, 1972).

to indicate a relationship with the transcendent or Holy.

As countless studies have shown, the largest percentage of the time and energy of clergy, and the consequent demand placed on key lay leaders, goes into the administration of the organizational life of a church.[5] The inertia of the social system is enormous. Critics who say that to pay attention to these factors is to reduce the Gospel to behavioral science do not understand that such system dynamics are the fountain out of which flows the secularizing, folk religious currents in church life—they must not be ignored. There is a danger because of the power of these forces to become all-consuming, a danger that is not obviated by repression or ignorance. The church is a laughable, befuddled institution when some of its leaders preach social action, give funds to empower the disenfranchised, and march in social action demonstrations, while it continues to conduct its own business by standards and practices that the ordinary member experiences as sexist, racially discriminatory, or indifferent to human need. Many leaders at work in the local congregation understand this dilemma. What they need and what many have developed are ways of moving beyond analysis to modifying the conduct of church life so that it does not stand as a denial of life and as a denial of the symbols it is to represent.

The way to be free is not to ignore the forces that chain and bind but to discern these principalities and powers. Langdon Gilkey writes: "The salvation of the church that has almost lost its Lord lies not in forgetting Him, but in finding Him again in its life. If that is to be possible, however, we must be free to experiment, not only with our theological language and our forms of mission and service, but even more with the structures of church life and organization which we have inherited from an age whose customs and spiritual forms were vastly different from our own."[6] What Gilkey is saying here is essentially correct. The recovery of the Holy is not solely or simply a matter of semantic discourse. Our language and our forms of service

---

[5]James D. Anderson, *To Come Alive* (New York: Harper & Row, 1973).
[6]Langdon Gilkey, *How the Church Can Minister to the World Without Losing Itself* (New York: Harper & Row, 1964).

are inextricably bound together in the web of church life and organization. The skill and wisdom to take the journey Gilkey prescribes involve understanding church life—the actualized psychological contracts and the functional covenant relationship.

A Roman Catholic theologian, David Tracy, has provided some basic insight into this theological task of correlating word and experience in the context of church life. Tracy proceeds from the assumption that the two principal sources for theology are human experience and language, and the words and symbols of the Christian tradition. To describe the religious dimension of everyday life Tracy uses the concept of "limit." Limit situations are those moments when an individual is made to realize the limits to our human situation. The experience can be positive, as in an ecstatic moment of joy and creativity, or negative, as in grief, guilt, or bereavement. All of these situations take us to the horizons of everyday life and reveal to us experiences which cannot be adequately explained and whose reality is touched only by the language and image of metaphor, myth, symbol, and poem. "That limit world of final closure to our lives now faces us with a starkness we cannot shirk and manages to disclose to us our basic existential faith or unfaith in life's very meaningfulness."[7] To the question of the meaning of life Tracy suggests that Scripture has as its referent a particular mode of being in the world, a way of living by faith in the known presence of a God whose love has no limits.

Tracy's work helps us to see that one of the basic tasks of theological leadership is to provide the settings and the climate of trust so that people may experience the limit conditions of life. For God to be known it is as important for the religious dimension of life to be known as it is for Biblical exposition to occur. The normal structures, processes, and experiences of the local church must expose rather than hide the horizon of life.

The church has been a frequent critic of American funeral customs. The basic thrust of the critique has been that the experience of death is lost through the palliatives and disguises

---

[7]David Tracy, *Blessed Rage for Order* (New York: Seabury, 1975).

of normal funeral practices. In the name of a Christian understanding of death the church has campaigned for less expensive and more realistic burial customs.

Many of the usual practices of congregational life obscure the limit experiences of anxiety, guilt, loneliness, and despair as surely as a mortician rearranging the features of a cold corpse. Church consultant John C. Harris tells the story of Messiah Church, a large suburban congregation in which the leadership had grown apathetic and without purposeful direction. Messiah had a vigorous period of growth in the fifties. The congregation's vitality ebbed in the middle sixties as it experienced an erosion in numbers and corporate spirit. What makes Messiah particularly interesting is the extraordinary number of efficiently run efforts its talented leadership mounted to try to reverse the trend. In an eight-year period the church was reorganized four times. A whole series of well planned programs were launched including a family calling program, new formats for Sunday worship and a series of house communions and Bible study groups. Each spring the church board went off for a two-day planning retreat. Young and vigorous assistant ministers were hired. The Sunday school was revamped through the aid of expert consultants. None of these efficiently run, well thought out programs changed the continued decline of Messiah's ministry. What went wrong? Why did such an extensive series of leadership efforts fail?

As Harris reflected on the Church of the Messiah he saw the problem as fear. Messiah's leaders were dominated by fears of interpersonal confrontation, personal criticism, and self examination. The leadership had built strong norms to support objectivity, rationality, and polite problem solving. Messiah was spiritually committed to smooth, anxiety free, bureaucratic functioning.

From both a theological and an organizational stance effective ministry leadership requires organizational practices which move into, rather than away from, the limit experiences of life. How can one sustain the experience of the fear of God if the settings of congregational life teach the suppresion of fear?

One of the most practical and attainable leadership objectives is to make it acceptable to engage in a searching, truthful evaluation of church life and practice. At one of Messiah's annual goal-setting conferences a member of the board asked if the board could talk some about the climate and conduct of its meetings. His question was met by silence and then another board member spoke saying, "Great idea. We can all get on our couches, do touchie-feelies, and stare at our navels. You can lead us, how about it?"[8]

Ordained and lay leaders cannot allow norms such as this to exist if the primary task of faith development is to occur. A congregation that exists without stress, anxiety, and strong emotion will end up substituting a stale, bland folk religion for the Gospel. Leaders can work for limit experience in church life through their own behavior and through a watchful eye on the climate of the congregation. Leaders who are open to criticism and who can live with the anxiety of powerful emotions model behavior for others.

Once a year, perhaps at an annual overnight conference, do an audit of your congregation's human and emotional climate. Do not rely on surveys and questionaires. There is no substitute for face to face conversation.

The following steps will usually facilitate honest, important conversation.

1. Give people time alone to write individual answers to your questions.

2. Ask people to pair and then to share their answers. Ask each pair to write down their responses.

3. Return the pairs to the larger group and post the responses. These reports become the basis for discussion and identification of priority issues.

There are many variations on this process, but it almost always helps to give people time to reflect and write alone before group discussion of critical, personal issues. The use of paper or chalkboard allows everyone to follow the course of the discussion.

---

[8]John C. Harris *Stress, Power and Ministry* (Washington D.C.: Alban Institute, 1977).

All of the following areas of inquiry have proved to be useful and important issues to audit.

1. Is reflection on one's individual religious pilgrimage a valued congregational activity? The answer is *no* in many churches; in others the answer is *yes* only for those who can witness to the party line.

2. Is corporate reflection on the impact, the actual transforming influence of congregational life, honored, valued, and performed? Ask if it is ever done. Ask newcomers, those who have not yet learned the "ways," what they are learning from church life.

3. What stories do we tell about ourselves? Who are the congregation's heroes and heroines? What is remembered, told, and related about the congregation, the sacrifices, the moments of dedication, the "mountain top" experiences? Every local church has a verbal tradition of its own scripture, its own myths, which gives meaning to the ongoing life of the congregation. We revere the Bible for the depths of wisdom, the expressions of love and justice caught in the remembered traditions of a people. Do we honor the remembered traditions of our own particular covenant community so as to hear within them the call to repentence and the judgment of God? We are struck by how seldom congregational planning and evaluation efforts tap into these oral traditions.

4. To what degree can the congregation tolerate differences? Do the processes by which people are involved respect the possibility of differing psychological contracts? And covenants?

5. Does membership in the church simply bring more busyness and activity, or does it instead provide space on the edge of the normal rounds of life?

Questions such as these are simply ways of posing the issues of whether our church has become just a social fellowship club or, in contrast, a situation of Christian communities squarely judged by scripture and tradition.

6. Is it acceptable to express affection or anger in the course of a church meeting? There are no shortcuts to face-to-face conversation. Surveys and questionnaires can elicit some infor-

mation in the area of psychological contract; they do a very inadequate job in the area of covenant and communitas.

Leadership and Problem Solving

A recent article in the *Harvard Business Review* described with great clarity what effective managers actually do every day. The description is both practical and useful. Managers engaged in three kinds of activity. The first area involved basic interpersonal relationships, the second with the gathering and transmission of information, and the third with the decision-making processes of their organization. The formal authority vested in a manager gives rise to the specific interpersonal roles, which in turn lead to the key communication roles, which in turn make the manager central in the decisions that must be made. The specific role activities are diagrammed in Figure 7.[9]

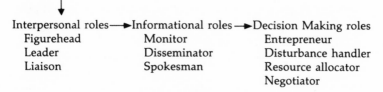

Formal authority and status

Interpersonal roles ⟶ Informational roles ⟶ Decision Making roles

Interpersonal roles	Informational roles	Decision Making roles
Figurehead	Monitor	Entrepreneur
Leader	Disseminator	Disturbance handler
Liaison	Spokesman	Resource allocator
		Negotiator

Figure 7. The Manager's Roles.

Clergy should be pleased to know that managers in business spent 12 percent of their time on ceremonial duties and that they considered such effort as signing diplomas and handing out awards as valuable to a smoothly running organization. The managers strongly favored verbal, face-to-face conversation; only 13 percent of their mail was of specific use. Managers don't leave meetings or hang up the telephone in order to get back to work, because such activities in fact constitute their work.

---

[9]Henry Mintzberg, "The Manager's Job: Folklore and Fact," *Harvard Business Review,* July–August 1975, vol. 53, no. 4. Copyright © 1975 by the President and Fellows of Harvard College; all rights reserved.

Finally, the article clarifies some of the specific skills a manager should know, contrasting skill learning with cognitive learning. Skills such as "developing peer relationships, carrying out negotiations, motivating subordinates, resolving conflicts, establishing information networks and subsequently disseminating information, making decisions in conditions of extreme ambiguity, and allocating resources" are needed by managers both in and out of the church. Skills cannot be learned from the pages of a book. Like playing tennis or swimming, management skills require constant practice. Therefore, introspection about one's work is essential for continued on-the-job learning. We have emphasized in this book the need for a model for the management of ministry so that such reflection might take place.

A key skill underlying the several managerial roles and one that greatly aids in the identification of other needed skills is that of problem solving. The acquisition of a new skill passes through four stages:

Unskilled   (1) Unconscious incompetence
             (2) Conscious incompetence
             (3) Conscious competence

Proficient   (4) Unconscious competence

Most church leaders are unconsciously incompetent in their problem-solving skills. Although they have heard the term and perhaps read an article on problem solving, they are not aware of their lack of proficiency. They are like swimmers flailing the water and causing a lot of commotion with little progress, yet having no sense of being incompetent swimmers. No one is a good problem solver by accident of birth. Skills must be consciously practiced until they become second nature.

The steps in an adequate problem-solving process, along with the conditions needed for the process to be effective, are:

1.   *Accept.* The essential, initial step of owning the problem. Involved is a clear decision to take on responsibility for the concern. Do not be misled because the group is discussing an issue of mutual concern. One reason such discussions persist without action is that the group has

never decided that it is the accountable body for the concern in question. The group may feel it has the responsibility to advise, question, warn or, suggest. The real issue is whether the group accepts responsibility for the work to be done.

Example: Ask the group to decide by vote or consensus if it accepts responsibility for the concern.

"We have talked before about the lack of youth in the church. Are you ready to put it on our agenda so that we can get to the bottom of this and do something about it?"

2. *Identify.* This is the process of surfacing the many elements of the concern. What is it that is bothering us and how do we see it from our several perspectives? This step involves compilation rather than analysis. As you compile viewpoints on the concern you will notice that people will almost always have differing views regarding the nature of the concern.

    Example: Ask each person to list the three most important elements of the issue as he or she sees it. Collect the answers and make a master list for all to see, discuss, and complete.

    "We had a good youth program when we had an assistant minister."

    "We have all gotten older. I wonder how many youth are actually in the church?"

    "The minister needs to give youth work higher priority."

    "The real problem is that we aren't getting any young families."

    "Our worship service has no appeal for teen-agers."

3. *Analyze.* What is the web of relationships among all of the elements of the concern? Contrast, compare, weight the different factors which comprise the issue. What you are trying to do is see the whole concern and the relationship of its many parts. Your analysis should give you a clear picture of the present situation, the desired situation, and the forces at work in the gap between what is and what is desired.

    Example: Use paper or chalkboard with arrows,

numbers, lines, and lists so that you get a graphic representation of the concern. One particularly useful method is a modification of a technique called force field analysis. This method of analysis has five steps.

    a. Briefly state the present situation. "We have 20 members, age 16 to 25, all inactive."

    b. Briefly state the desired situation. "Increase our active youth membership."

    c. List all of the factors or forces which impede movement toward the desired state. Do this by examining what you have learned of the situation and identifying the restraints and hindrances present.

    d. In a similar fashion, list all of the factors or forces which support movement toward the desired goal. Looking at all that we know of the situation, what are the present forces driving us toward the outcome desired?

When you have completed steps *a* through *d,* you should have a chart which looks like the following diagram.

(+) *Increased youth membership*	(−) *Twenty inactive youth*
Education committee wants action.	Worship service lacks appeal to youth.
Sue and Tom are competent youth leaders.	We are set in our ways.
Program dollars are available.	The neighborhood has changed, the new families are not like us.
Many new neighborhood families have teen-agers.	Minister has not given priority to youth work.
	Most of present membership lives several miles from the church, is not part of the neighborhood.

    e. The fifth step in this process of analysis is to identify the most important factors in the present situation. Quite often removing some of the obstacles or restraints is the easiest and best way to achieve change. Be alert to the possibility that your analysis may give you such a different picture from the one that you started with that you will end up changing the nature of your concern.

4. *Define.* This is the act of specifying one or a set of defined, workable problems that have emerged from the process of identification and analysis. You are choosing an aspect of the concern which seems critical to its resolution and which seems within your power to change.

Example: In this instance the analysis helped the group to see that its concern for youth was an outgrowth of a larger issue. The neighborhood had changed and the church was not attracting new families. With this new concern the group once again moved through the first three steps of the problem solving process. In step four it was able to define several workable problems, one of which was "we must let the neighborhood know we are here and that we welcome new members." A problem well defined is a problem nearly solved. It is then a workable problem.

5. *Search.* Producing ideas is probably the most natural phase of problem solving. The usual danger is that new ideas get elaborated before the problem has ever been defined. Without reinventing the wheel, the point is to describe creative and high quality alternative paths toward problem resolution.

Example: Brainstorm (list without critical comment) as many suggestions as the group can fruitfully produce. Find out what others have done to solve a similar problem. Ask an expert for advice.

6. *Select.* This is the exercise of judgment about the best way to proceed. Ministry problems do not lead to quantifiable cost-benefit procedures for selection. Once again, the more adequate and refined the problem definition, the easier the selection process.

Example: Give form to what you think is the best alternative. Do this by listing the tasks which must be accomplished in order to carry out the idea. Schedule the tasks. Now does the idea still seem feasible? What you have done is to test your idea by looking ahead to see what is involved. If the alternative chosen holds up under this scrutiny, you will also have gotten a head start on the planning which must be done to implement your solution.

From this decision point, the group proceeds to implementation and evaluation, which, in effect, are the beginning of a new problem solving cycle. Some conditions or ground rules are necessary for this process to work effectively:

1.   The Black-Cloud Rule. This rule states that every problem is really a set or system of problems. The phrase *the problem is* should be outlawed. Avoid looking for *the* problem and instead work to unpack the mess into a set of defined, workable problems. Whatever the initial concern, it is simply a black cloud, which, after identification and analysis, is revealed to be made up of a whole field of forces. When people talk about "the problem we are having," they usually mean "the mess (the system of problems) we are experiencing."

2.   The Workable-Problem Rule. A particularly useful understanding of a defined problem is that "a problem is a deviation between what *should* be happening and what *actually* is happening that is important enough to make someone think the deviation ought to be corrected.[10] You don't have a defined, workable problem until you know both what is presently and what ought to be. It is not uncommon to see a group energetically brainstorming ideas or enthusiastically latching onto an innovation proffered by some influential member, without any clarity regarding the present situation or consensus regarding a desired outcome.

3.   The Cycle-Back Rule. If you run into trouble moving through the steps of this process and seem to bog down

---

[10]Charles H. Kepner and Benjamin B. Tregoe, *The Rational Manager* (New York: McGraw-Hill, 1965).

or are unable to gain any perspective on the black cloud troubling you, *stop* what you are doing and move back to the preceding step. Check out the clarity of that step and, if still befuddled, move back yet another step, and so on. The worth of this rule is quite apparent when we note the many times a group will engage in discussion of a concern that, in fact, no one in the group actually owns. At other times the cycle-back rule reveals that the issues under discussion are actually red herrings because people's real concerns seem too sensitive to air.

Problem solving is the elixir of management skills. It is the skill that can help to identify the other skills that need improvement. It is the continuous skill of the roles of relationship builder, communicator, and decision maker. The tasks of authentic spiritual direction, efficient organization, and effective leadership in the building and maintaining of psychological contracts and faithful covenants are constant and complex. Count on things going wrong, mistakes happening, and people becoming upset. In the management of ministry such mistakes are opportunities for increased communication, the improvement of our capacities to solve problems, and the clarification of our corporate gifts.

10

Mission and Ministry

Core mission or primary task is the element of the ministry system of the local church that is a measure of the integration and function of the system as a whole. It is the way we understand the essence of what we are doing. Ideal core missions will be as varied as the theology and philosophy of the individuals involved. As we have stated in citing Avery Dulles in Chapter 6, five quite distinct historical Christian traditions can shape primary task.

The persisting, dominant task of a local church is unlikely to fit smoothly within any one of Dulles' categories. By using an analytical exercise based on Dulles' *Models of the Church,* we have helped a number of church groups clarify their own perspective on the identity and mission of the church. Even within a single congregation of one denomination the range and variety of answers is startling. It is no wonder that many church conversations end in a frustrating babble of tongues. The lack of common assumptions and perspectives demands that there be some sorting out and clarification of underlying assumptions before intelligent discussion is possible.

The management of ministry requires an assessment both of what the primary task is and of what the church thinks it should be. Achieving clarity and consensus about either or both of these questions is a formidable task, and answers are sadly lacking. In economics we could look back to 1900 and, in retrospect, see the primary task decision to use handcraft skills to turn leather into buggy whips. Such clarity is not available to the local church. Moreover, when it involves interpersonal relations and sacred ritual, the analysis of primary task is much more than a matter of measurement.

There is one organization development tool that can be helpful, called *open systems planning.* Open systems planning can guide the work of a several-month effort to clarify primary task concerns, or it can be utilized in a single weekend as a quick probe. Open systems planning is focused upon relationships rather than goals, and forces an examination of the behavior between the congregation and its key groupings and between the congregation and the main elements in the community. For this reason it is a more practical and useful tool than the normal goal-oriented planning process.

Step 1—Clarifying intended core mission, based upon discussion of our history, our resources, our values, and the nature of the community we serve. A preliminary consensus is reached regarding the intended primary task. The history of the church is an especially valuable asset in this discussion. The patterns of the past are likely to be most revealing of prior primary task performance. The history is a picture of values in action. What was happening in the community and in the church during past peak eras? What would you say was the identity of the church during those eras? Has the community changed? From your history may come the best guidance for the central task of the present and the future. This step, like many others in the open systems planning process, can be pulled out and worked on by a single task force for several weeks. Alternatively you can rely on the present knowledge of the planning group and move expeditiously through the steps without the benefit of homework and task force assignments.

Step 2—Identifying the present demand system.
 a. Identify and list the domains that are making demands on the church, such as the immediate neighborhood around the church, single young adults, the elderly retired, denominational agencies, municipal zoning laws, and transient indi-

gents. From your standpoint as leaders of the church, what are the cliques, groups, organizations, laws, environmental forces, and economic realities which are making demands upon you.

b. Specify the demands from each domain. Try to be as clear and specific as possible in the way each domain would answer the statement, "We want you, the local church, to do and give and be this to us." For instance, what are the demands placed upon you by the synod, or the diocese, or the presbytery, or the district? What do they want you to do? What do they want you to give? What do they want you to be?

c. Identify the church's present response to each of the demands. List the specific ways you respond to a domain. Do not neglect to list any demands you may make of a domain. If possible you may want to do some investigation and ask some of the representatives of a domain what they perceive your response to be. Rate the quality of your responses. Suppose you have identified as a domain five new families who have joined in the last six months.

Their demands you see as:

to give them a place to belong and make friends

to give their children an enjoyable, productive, church school experience

to be a place of pastoral support as they seek to make the transition to a new community

to get to know the minister as a pastor

Your response you see as:

a class for new members

an atmosphere of openness to strangers

regular church school classes

a home visit from a lay calling committee

a home visit from the minister

placement on the church mailing list.

You note that though the Sunday school exists, it is often neither enjoyable nor productive. The new member class is more of an orientation to the denomination than a group for pastoral support.

It is difficult to be comprehensive, clear, and accurate in specifying the present demand system, as outlined in tasks a, b, and c. For example, one congregation quite correctly identified the fact that they had a sizable and growing group of retired elderly, and also that the neighborhood contained a large number of elderly, mostly female, shut-ins, who needed nutritional assistance and opportunity for fellowship and human contact. As responses the church created a "super-sixties" club, a "meals on wheels" program, and a daily lunch program at the church. What this response created was a "social service" approach to the elderly. The complaint was voiced that "if you turn sixty-five and don't want to sit around and play dominoes with the super-sixties, there doesn't seem to be a place for you here." Many of the elderly retired members of the congregation had been active church members in other communities. They were still healthy, vigorous members of society, often holding a variety of important business and civic posts despite their formal retirement. What these people said they wanted from the church varied little from the demands of their middle years. Instead of being offered positions of responsibility and active roles in church life, many of these people felt they were being treated as disabled and indigent.

Identifying domains, their demands and the response, is a process that can involve extensive interviews and prolonged investigation. Most congregations will uncover a range of demands so extensive that it leads to the awareness of a new problem. What tasks ought to be dominant among the many choices? Churches suffer from trying to be all things to all people. The minister in particular can accomplish little if he or she rushes in every direction at once. Time management experts often advise that seventy to eighty per-cent of what you must do is contained in one or two of the thirty to forty tasks you might list to accomplish in a given period. The list of tasks for a minister or a church is so lengthy it is never completed. The secret is knowing which of the tasks are critical or primary and seeing that those are accomplished first. A clear identity is a vital condition of church growth and church vitality. The means of achieving a clear identity is to clarify and carry out one or two dominant tasks.

The next steps in open systems planning are designed to achieve the desired primary task clarity and accomplishment.

Step 3—Projecting the present situation into the future. The task of this step is to consider what the situation will be like in three to five years if nothing changes in the present demand system. It is important, and relatively easy, to project demographic patterns, taking into account inflation, mobility, and aging. If you do not change or improve your present responses what will be the long term consequences?

Step 4—Extrapolating desired future demands. If we were carrying out our primary task, what would the various domains be asking of us in three to five years? Notice the reorienting effect of this question rather than one focused on our own goals. The whole open systems planning process is sharply focused upon the demands the environment makes upon us and our responses.

Step 5—Deciding strategy and next steps. The final step is the creation of a plan of action in answer to the question, "What steps must we take in order to bring each particular domain to the point of demanding that we perform our primary task?" This will elicit a set of goals to alter the relationships.

We think, for example, of one of the most rapidly growing and interesting churches we know. A few years ago it was a typical congregation, undistinguished from most other churches of its denomination. The minister and other lay leaders identified new young families moving into the neighborhood as a key domain. They saw their primary task as the provision of a Sunday morning of worship and education keyed to family concerns. They gave this task precedence over all else. Within two years they began to grow at a rapid rate, attracting more and more of the families in the community. Creative and able leaders were set free by primary task clarity.

Establishing a distinct, appropriate, authoritative mission is an increasingly difficult task for the local church. It is no longer sufficient just to open the doors and hold regular services of worship. Both in and out of the church a wide variety of agencies, groups, and individuals demand that the church respond to their situation and needs. Each seems to say, we know what the church ought to be and do. History and theology no longer provide a convincing answer to the direction of the mission of the church. Achieving a clear identity has become an increasing rarity for a local church. Sometimes it is accomplished by the charisma and force of a few insightful leaders. In other situations a process such as open systems planning becomes a compass for the needed direction finding. In all too many cases neither happens, and the local church simply continues to carry out its usual activities, ebbing and flowing with the currents of its segment of American culture.

Another useful means of clarifying primary task is to see where the leadership is expending its energies. What are the tasks that involve the leaders, both ordained and lay? Those tasks will fall into three areas: organizational management, associational leadership, and spiritual direction.

It is our observation that these tasks are distributed in some characteristic patterns. A dominant pattern is that of the organized, active, associational congregation—the pattern of many suburban congregations that emphasize fellowship and belonging (see Figure 8).

This form of congregation is typified by the burnt-out volunteer worker who has spent countless hours in church activity and now, years later, wonders why. Such churchs typically put great emphasis upon expanding the circle of involved persons. What escapes notice is that the circle can be enlarged indefinitely without altering the proportional distribution of task energy. Lack of primary task clarity usually leads by default to an overemphasis upon the tasks associated with organizational maintenance and member belonging. We know of a

Figure 8. How Leaders Expend Their Energies in a Typical Suburban Congregation.

new mission congregation set up to emphasize the dual tasks of spiritual development and social witness. It is apparent from watching the struggles of this fledgling church that the tasks of organizing a congregation, attracting new members, raising money, keeping peace with the landlord, paying a salary, and governing the association have a built-in inertia that almost automatically gives these duties a primacy that was never intended in the congregation's charter. Perhaps it is for this reason that many efforts to revitalize local churches end up as motivational campaigns to enlarge the core of involved leaders, or simply rearrange the balance between energies devoted to organizational and associational concerns.

Churchwide movements such as Faith at Work, Marriage Encounter, and Cursillo[1] often have a dramatic impact upon the local church because they serve to greatly increase the slice of lay leadership energy going into spiritual development and associational concerns. At the same time their "movement" qualities, stemming from a powerful shared experience, serve to

---

[1]*Cursillo* (Spanish for *short course*) is an intense and highly structured conference experience of teaching and community. It has been particularly influential in the Roman Catholic and Episcopal churches.

bring new vigor to the belonging, associational side of church life.

This movement approach to increasing task emphasis upon spiritual direction is not for every minister or congregation. The messianic vigor of a movement can lead to neglect of the other tasks of leadership. Conflicts arise when conversion to "our way" seems to be a directive rather than an invitation. Nevertheless, many congregations need to shift the balance of leadership energy. More clergy need to be able to say, as the Rev. Dennis Maynard has, "I spend 40 to 50 per cent of my time doing spiritual direction. I help people find books to read, work on their prayer life, examine their consciences, and learn how to do Bible study properly."[2] This clergyman runs spiritual growth groups for members and then encourages them to start their own prayer and Bible-study groups. Thus, once again, the tasks of developing fellowship and enhancing faith development are simultaneously strengthened.

A good first step is for the minister to exert leadership by example. Pick up your appointment calendar and set aside time each week—time for yourself and family, for your own spiritual growth. Schedule time to be used in spiritual development activities with the congregation. At first you may not know what you will be doing in either of these new areas. Don't let your own need for clarity prevent you from leaving time open—this space must be protected from being shoved out of your schedule. It is not free time to be filled in when your week is crowded but time that is scheduled in accord with your primary leadership task.

Use the space for yourself for prayer, meditation, training in spiritual direction, study, and recreation. Let others know what you are doing and why.

Use the space devoted to congregational spiritual development to:

Start a prayer group or Bible-study group.

---

[2]Interview with the Rev. Dennis Maynard in *The Episcopalian,* October 1977, vol. 142, no. 10.

Start an adult education group focused on faith development issues.

Seriously investigate one of the spiritual movement groups such as Cursillo.

Help individuals to pray and study.

The idea of all this is not to neglect or downgrade the importance of efficiency in organization or the building of fellowship and community. A recent congregational conflict that we know of stemmed directly from the fact that the minister had so neglected the administrative aspects of congregational life that people were eventually incensed by organizational mishaps, and congregational involvement diminished, despite the minister's obvious interest in spiritual issues.

By the example of his or her own leadership, the minister can move toward increasing the weight of spiritual development in the life of the congregation. Some ministers who have done this describe the difference as "not trying to kill myself to make the congregation go but taking more time for the things that really count."

Fortunately, the Christian church has allowed space for reform movements in almost every new generation. These movements, often spreading with the vigor of a forest fire, have served to briefly purge, cleanse, and renew by their usual exaggerated emphasis upon some element of the church's mission. The management of ministry implies that with thoughtful, concerted effort a more routine, ongoing course of integrity and Christian service might be possible. We do know it can happen because we have seen it happen. That it seldom happens is the reason for this book.

11

An Integrated Framework for Ministry

An integrated theological and sociological framework offers a systematic process by which a congregation continuously utilizes its understanding of God and his activity in the world, as well as knowledge of its social context, in making decisions about the church's role in relating people to God. Each local church, usually without conscious awareness of the theological implications, makes decisions about its role and acts upon them—many of them each year. The crucial question is whether it makes the decisions deliberately, thoughtfully, and intentionally, in such a way that the church does not lose sight of its total task in its particular setting, that later decisions are consistent with earlier ones, and that the basis of the theology is rooted in apostolic Christianity rather than apocryphal folk religion. It is not enough for the decisions to lead to action; they must be grounded in the church's primary task. A conception of the church's purpose is not sufficient; it must undergird every decision and be effectively implemented.

This book describes the components of an integrated framework for the ministry of local churches. We have pointed to the systematic interrelationship of the four components of ministry, which, taken together, provide definition and guidelines of the church's function in society. We have suggested the pertinent questions to be raised and the character of the answers to be sought with regard to each component and at each stage in the ministry process. It is our hope that ministers and churches have found help in coming to terms with God's revelation, in working out and using their own terminology and concepts to express their faith, and in carrying out their own studies to determine the distinctive character of their communities.

The essential ingredients of an intergrated framework for the church in contemporary America may be summarized as follows:

1. The subject matter of the church is religion. Christianity offers its answer to the questions of religion. It is not enough for the church to concern itself only with the faith which it proclaims. Its faith participates in the nature of religion itself.

Religion may be defined as the inescapability of ultimate concerns. It is an emotional and intellectual quest for that which is ultimate, dependable and capable of imbuing life with meaning, direction and release from that which binds. God is that about which a person is ultimately concerned, that upon which one feels absolutely dependent, that which is believed to be the source of meaning, that which is trusted to provide for the person's needs. Within one's religious framework a person feels and expresses feelings about his or her ultimate concern, thinks and constructs doctrines about it and works out acceptable ways to act in relation to it. To accomplish its purpose in the world, the church must understand this essential nature of religion and the diversity of religious quests (the gods, rites, values, goals and methods).

2. The content of the church's concern with religion is the Christian faith. Christianity is a religion in which people for two thousand years in every part of the world have found an acceptable way of understanding and ordering their feelings about their ultimate concerns, of making sense of the world, of finding meaning for their lives, and of expressing their faith and hope about life after death. In each age the church has to come to terms with the faith that it has received and reinterpret it. It has to re-experience God as creator and sustainer of life revealed in Hebrew tradition, as just and loving Father revealed in the birth and life of Jesus Christ, as redeemer accomplished in Christ's death, and as continuing presence and comforter through the Holy Spirit. It has to study and interpret the Bible as the primary source of God's revelation and appropriate its teachings about the sanctity of human life and love of neighbor.

It has to establish goals for seeking righteousness, working for justice, living in favor with God and neighbor, and sharing the faith with others. And it has to institute activities of worship, prayer, observance of sacraments, and obedience in daily life to achieve its goals.

3. The church must understand the nature and task of the Christian church and local congregations in order to be clear about its own identity and purpose. The Christian church is the mystical body of people in all ages and in all denominations who have accepted, practiced and found meaning for their lives in Christianity. In each generation Christians receive the faith, develop it for their time, share it with others and pass it on to succeeding generations. They band together in redemptive fellowships under the Lordship of Christ to hear the Word of God, to receive the Sacraments, and to challenge, support, and comfort one another in their daily lives. Each local church must decide how these tasks can be accomplished efficaciously in its situation.

The congregation is the primary unit of the church. It is in local churches in local communities, through fellowships of people who are like-minded in religious faith and who have accepted Jesus Christ as Lord and Savior that people are related to God. It is there that believers covenant together to participate in events which recall and manifest their common hope, to hear and gather sustenance from their common tradition, to strengthen the tradition through the common exploration of the meaning of life and their part in it, to participate in rites which celebrate the benevolence and assistance of their God, to share their faith with their neighbors, to prepare for their servant role in the community and to be energized to operate in the world with purpose and strength.

In the daily routines of work, school, recreation, travel, relaxation and sundry activities, the disciples of Christ witness to their faith, exemplify the values which emanate from Biblical teachings, and lobby for, support and participate in activities which promote righteousness, justice and equality of opportunity for all people to find meaning and fulfillment of life. For Christians, meaning is found in life as it is facilitated for others. As the faithful go about their lives in the assurance that life is meaningful and that they have a contribution to make to the world, there are times when they go aside into the church. The church must understand the ultimate concerns that bring people to it, their expressed and unexpressed needs, and how it can facilitate their relating those concerns to God.

4. In the particular setting in time and space, the church must seek to understand the ultimate concerns of its people and relate those concerns to the ultimacy and dependability of God; that is, correlate people's needs and God's answer. The primary task of the local church as a social institution varies by community—by the needs, customs and culture of the people who live there—although the basic meaning system of the church is the same at different times and places. The church structures itself appropriately to relate the concerns of the people to the revelation and judgment of God.

5. As it carries out its correlating and catalytic function—its primary task—the church performs multiple services and becomes involved in diverse activities. As the church understands life in its community, as it familiarizes itself with the multiple relationships of its members and constituents, as it concentrates its efforts on managing their reliance upon God and development to independent participation in human encounters in which their Christian faith and values are manifested, it accomplishes its primary task. When it succumbs to the temptation to narrow its focus to the spiritual dimension of persons and loses sight of the totality of their social relationships, its ministry is irrelevant to the hurts and conditions of mankind. When it allows people to withdraw from the world into the church as a sanctuary, which offers respite from the demands of life or a haven where people can opt out, change does not occur and individuals are sent back into the world no better prepared for living than when they came. In this instance worshippers avoid contact with the church as it ceases to provide a facilitating environment for life and only reminds them of their weakness and fractured condition. Finally, when the church substitutes social and community activities for its primary task of managing the reliance upon God and development to strength and independence of its people, it is covering up, or trying to make up for, its failure to perform its primary task. In

this case participants in the church are held in a state of dependency upon the church and prohibited from returning to the challenges, opportunities and responsibilities of the "real" world.

6. The primary task of the church is to receive people as they are, enable them to submit their lives in dependence upon the ground and source of their being, and return to society renewed and strengthened for participation in other social institutions. Apart from the chance involvement of one or more of its members in another social institution of the community, however, the church has no direct relationship with other social institutions. The consequence of this division of roles has serious consequences for society. Each social institution or organization develops its own principles and values for functioning in the world. The political, economic, educational, legal, cultural, health, and welfare organizations operate autonomously. This condition increases the multiplicity of distinct patterns of relationships which segment the lives of the people who participate in them or call upon them for services. Each institution is cut off from benefiting from the accomplishments and insights of the others. The church must understand the character and tasks of other societal institutions and groups, how it interrelates appropriately with them and they with each other, and the limits of its own responsibility.

7. The end of the church's efforts is the fulfillment of human lives and the creation of a society in which love and justice prevail. Some of the activity that goes on in the church enables people to cope with life, but it is not related to the church's primary task and it is not apostolic Christianity. It offers comfort or escape for the time, but it does not issue in changed lives that are equipped to make a difference in societal relationships.

As Christians live and participate in society, they have a responsibility to bring their Christian faith and values to bear upon relationships. The church must prepare them to initiate, lobby for, and work toward a society in which just and loving relationships predominate. Where folk religion is expressed in Christian symbols, as is true throughout American society, the church must identify with the needs of people caught up in the folk religion and attempt to help them interpret their needs more realistically in terms of the faith of the apostles. It must do so without expecting them to turn their backs on the folk religion before they have understood how the apostolic faith can satisfy their needs.

All of life is the church's concern. The task of the church in the community is to enable people to find direction and meaning for the whole of their lives, to provide a value system for their diverse relationships in society, and to relate them to God who alone is able to provide strength for the task.

At present there is a pseudo-dichotomy and tension in the church between those who emphasize personal salvation and those who stress the church's responsibility for social involvement. The arguments on both sides are superfluous and without substance. Neither concern is significant except as it is related with the other. The critical concern for the church today is whether it will allow its constituents to escape from the world and remain in a state of dependency on the church, which has the effect of removing the church from involvement in the world; whether it will identify the church and the world so closely that members are expected to work out their own salvation by doing "good works" in the world; or whether it will receive people in their brokenness, relate them to the ultimate source of healing and wholeness, and return them to the world as reconstituted beings who can function in diversity and enable the same for their neighbors. The church must continually evaluate its ministry lest it become a closed system—operating apart from the world.

8. The success of the church is not measured, and its faithfulness cannot be evaluated by, institutional criteria. When people are allowed to withdraw into the church to get away from the world, the church measures success by the number of people who attend its activities. When participants are allowed to become dependent upon the church in order to find a place of service in the world or allow the church to dominate their social relationships, success is measured by the number of activities taking place in the church's building, the number participating, or the number served.

The church must gauge its success by the quality of lives

redeemed and the characteristics of the social milieu where those lives are lived. When the primary task of the church is perceived to be that of accepting people in weakness to return them to the world in strength, success is measured in terms of the quality of the lives that have been renewed. "The test of the Christian religion is whether the worship of God enables the worshipper to come to terms with the facts of life, and to seek to establish relationships with people so that the society which results enhances human dignity and does not devalue it. To express this in another way, the value of the Christian religion, in human terms at least, is not seen by its success in attracting worshippers, or in the number of converts, but by assessing whether the presence of a Christian institution within a society enables the members of that society (many of whom will not be church goers) to control and govern their lives according to love, peace, justice, righteousness and freedom."[1]

The measurement of success according to these criteria is always difficult and sometimes impossible. But why do churches need to be concerned with measuring their success? Some may feel the necessity of doing so because they are not sure of themselves or their primary task. Other churches may need quantitative tests to assuage their guilt for not performing the primary task.

The purpose of the church is to enable "members of society in their role as citizens to engage with the real human needs of their community, by helping them in their role as worshippers to realize their full humanity."[2] If the church is fulfilling this task it will not need to test it. The testimony of church members and non-church members alike will witness that God is at work in the church redeeming and renewing lives for the task of imparting meaning to all of life.

It is impossible at a given point in history to develop a framework appropriate for all time in every community. Even

---

[1]Bruce Reed, "The Task of the Church and the Role of Its Members" (London: The Grubb Institute, 1975, a paper based on the Keene Lecture delivered at Chelmsford Cathedral, England, November 1974), p. 8.
[2]*Ibid.*, p. 24.

theological frameworks become dated and irrelevant as social settings change and God's revelation is understood in new ways. Perhaps the one unchanging characteristic of the church is the necessity for it to reexamine continually its social environment, reinterpret its Faith even as it lives it, and develop new frameworks for relating the faith and the social environment.

The task of the local congregation is complex and continuous, but it is possible. The church cannot afford to become overwhelmed or incapacitated by it. As long as it recognizes the temporality and fluidity of its theology and the context in which it is shared, the church can draw aside from the ongoing theological and sociological processes at times to develop a framework for clarifying its mandate, rethinking its faith, and restudying the needs of the community. In that framework it can operate effectively and confidently, even as it continues its search for new wisdom and new data.

List of Related Books

The Nature of Religion

Becker, Ernest. *The Denial of Death.* New York: The Free Press, 1973.

Luckman, Thomas. *Invisible Religion.* New York: Macmillan, 1967.

Turner, Victor. *The Ritual Process.* Chicago: Aldine, 1970.

Westerhoff, John H. and Gwen Kennedy Neville. *From Generation to Generation.* Philadelphia: Pilgrim Press, 1974.

The Mission and Ministry of the Church

Dulles, Avery, S.J. *Models of the Church.* Garden City: Doubleday & Co., 1974.

Holmes, Urban T. *Ministry and Imagination.* New York: Seabury, 1976.

Niebuhr, H. Richard. *The Purpose of the Church and Its Ministry.* New York: Harper & Row, 1956.

Reed, Bruce. "The Task of the Church and the Role of its Members." Washington, D. C.: The Alban Institute, 1975.

Parish Life and Practice

Anderson, James D. *To Come Alive, A Proposal for Revitalizing the Local Church.* New York: Harper & Row, 1973.

Biersdorf, John, ed. *Creating an International Ministry.* Nashville: Abingdon, 1976.

Hoge, Dean R. *Division in the Protestant House.* Philadelphia: West-minster, 1976.

Jones, Ezra Earl. *Strategies For New Churches.* New York: Harper & Row, 1976.

Nouwen, Henri J. M. *The Wounded Healer.* Garden City: Double-day, 1972.

Organization and Management

Fiedler, Fred E. *A Theory of Leadership Effectiveness.* New York: McGraw Hill, 1967.

Kast, Fremont E., and James E. Rosenzweig. *Organization and Management.* New York: McGraw Hill, 1970.

Miller, Eric J., ed. *Task and Organization.* London: Wiley, 1976.

Porter, Lyman W., *et al. Behavior in Organizations.* New York: McGraw Hill, 1975.

The Growth of People and Groups

Bion, W. R. *Experiences in Groups.* New York: Basic Books, 1959.

Satir, Virginia. *Peoplemaking.* Palo Alto: Science & Behavior, 1972.

Index